My Great Life
With a Perfect Wife

CLEMENT VAUGHN SMITH, III

To Marshfield C.O.A.

Clem Smith

This memoir is dedicated to my wonderful wife, Franny. Thanks to the Creator, I was blessed with her presence for 60 years, 58 married and two years going together.

The cover photo was taken in 1996 by my son-in-law, Andy Walsh. He often noticed the unique and special connection Franny Girl and I had, and had the innate talent to capture it in this photo. He presented me with several framed pictures after Franny passed that captured our special looks. I treasure them all and extend my sincerest thanks to Andy for bringing back those memories.

Contents

Part 3: My Work Life

Part 4: More Years, More Stories

A GREAT LIFE
WITH A PERFECT WIFE

Preface

I'M CONVINCED I'VE BEEN GIFTED WITH DIVINE GUIDANCE throughout my life. I've been blessed with a great and interesting life. I have this strong belief because no one is that lucky. Also, I can't believe I was smart enough to always take the right path. Several times in my life there were unfortunate occurrences, which were painful and seemed wrong at the time, but led to improvement in my life, all thanks to the Creator.

PART ONE

MY EARLY LIFE

1936—Clement V. Smith III

CHAPTER I

The Early Years

THE 1930s WAS THE DEPTH OF THE GREAT DEPRESSION. Before my parents met, my dad was in school at the Virginia Military Institute in Lexington, Virginia. He studied electrical engineering. His family was wealthy, from Elkin, North Carolina, but they lost their wealth during The Great Depression. The story I heard was that my grandfather and his brother had major investments in Florida, most of which were with borrowed money. There were other contributing issues; it was truly a house of cards!

Dad was forced to leave school and find work. From stories of that time, he found work as a lineman on electrical utility systems. His father abandoned the family, never to be heard from again. Many, many years later, we found out where he'd been. His mother, due to the chaos in Elkin, had a nervous breakdown and ended up in the insane asylum. I have a memory of my Grandmother Smith. I think I was about four years old. I don't know where it was, but it was in Virginia. We went for a ride on the trolley. That was our only meeting.

I also remember knowing Dad was the oldest child and had a brother and sister. I remember meeting his brother, John, several times. Later in my adult years I met his sister, Virginia. Many years later while attending a Smith Family Reunion, I learned from a cousin there were two other younger sisters, whose names were unknown and what happened to them was a mystery.

When I was a young child, I recall Dad was the director of a Civilian Conservation Corps camp. This was a program set up by President Roosevelt to provide employment for young men. It provided food, shelter, and small pay. The program provided maintenance and improvement for national parks.

My mother, Grace Gorman, also came from a wealthy family. She had three sisters and a brother. Mom was the youngest. Her sisters were married to husbands who couldn't find work. My grandfather was their total support. He owned jewelry stores in Salisbury, North Carolina, but business was poor, which must have caused much stress. I never knew him; he died at age 56.

How my mother and father got together is a mystery. I don't know where they were married, but after doing so, they settled in the town of Buena Vista, Virginia, about eight miles from Lexington. It was in a valley in the mountains, a beautiful place. I was born in 1934, their first child. Dad and I shared the same name. I'm Clement Vaughn Smith III. From the very beginning I was called Vaughn by my family, probably so they could differentiate me from my father, plus I don't think my father really liked me having his name, even though naming me as such was a traditional thing. In school and at work I was always Clem.

My earliest memory is from when I was an infant, being tossed back and forth between my father and another man. Mom stood by and I was terrified! I can't say this actually happened, but I do have an irrational fear of heights, and a strong memory.

Early life in Buena Vista was normal and pleasant. There was church on Sunday and lots of playing in the neighborhood. Dad raised Pointers for bird hunting, so there were lots of dogs around. I also had pets. I remember a rooster, who later became a roaster, and a duck.

I recall Mom often played bridge with other ladies. I was probably around three or four years of age and amused myself for hours by
building houses of cards while the games went on.

Around this time Dad changed jobs. The story he told was that
he applied for a job as an engineer for the Bureau of Public Roads. To
be considered, he had to quit his job as Civilian Conservation Corps
Camp Director and take a test. There were three job openings, and
the top three scores would be chosen. Of the 165 people who took
the test, Dad was third. Years later, I remember Dad talking about
how, at the time, he never thought about the risk he took by leaving
his job to take the Bureau of Public Roads test. Somehow, he was
sure he wouldn't fail. After that, he worked on the Blue Ridge Park-
way, a scenic highway, as a construction engineer. Luckily, Buena
Vista was near this project, so we didn't have to move.

Around age five, life seemed good. I had friends I played with,
and we explored the woods and the foothills nearby. I participated
in all the normal activities for kids my age. At that time, Western
movies played in the theaters on Saturday afternoons. I went by
myself, and it cost a nickel or a dime. I have very fond memories of
those times.

Our family seemed relatively well off. We even had a part-time
maid. I think she did laundry and prepared occasional meals. Her
name was Ella: a nice, rather elderly black lady. Of course, in those
days there were no TVs or computers. I think we had a radio.

Buena Vista was a small town where life was pleasant and seemingly normal. Given the economic conditions at the time, one would
expect there would be many people down on their luck, but I can't
recall any poor folks: no bums, beggars or homeless whom one sees
today.

There were some folks much better off than we were. My parents
had some good friends, the Browns: a man and his wife, no children.
They lived on a large farm outside the town. The farmland was on a
river. It was low lying and may have flooded at times. The house was

a large, fancy, classic plantation house with a large barn for horses. They had several servants and I remember spending time there.

At some point, perhaps age six, I remember going to the public school and taking a test to see if I was ready for first grade. Apparently, I flunked and was held back a year. Other than that, my early life was pleasant and normal.

CHAPTER 2

The Crisis

WHEN I WAS AGE SIX, MY PARENTS GOT INTO BOOZE. I remember bathtub gin being prepared. One night, with both parents drunk, Dad started to beat up Mom. I grabbed the plunger from the bathroom and hit Dad with it in an attempt to stop him. It worked! He then punched me in the face and walked out. I didn't see him again until two or more years later.

After a short stay at some type of boarding house in Buena Vista, we stayed with Mom's sisters in Summerville, South Carolina, and Portsmouth, Virginia. We also lived in Salisbury, North Carolina, in boarding houses in two locations. Mom's mother, my Grandmother Gorman, also lived there in a different boarding house. She worked as a salesclerk at a department store and seemed to me to be a very cold and sad person.

Life in Black and White

My early life was mostly in the southern states. While racism was very active there, my experiences with black people centered more around the separation and segregation of the races. Even so, I never really processed it that way or gave it much thought at the time.

I remember when we lived in Summerville, South Carolina, with my aunt's family, we lived next door to a black family. In that house was a boy about my age. We became good friends. About one-quarter mile away his uncle had a pool hall and bar. He was a successful businessman, very nice as I recall.

Perhaps one-half mile away in the opposite direction was an estate, a very large house, on at least five acres surrounded by a chain link fence. A white family lived there. There was a boy close to my age, another playmate.

My preference was the black boy. I don't recall why this was, but he seemed a more solid friend. The fact his skin was darker than mine wasn't a factor for me in our friendship.

One situation occurred when I was eight or nine years old. We lived for a time in a development of hundreds of houses in Portsmouth, Virginia. It was outside the city, and I took the bus to go to the movies. On the bus ride I was seated in the white section. As the bus filled, there was standing room only. Next to my seat stood an elderly black lady. She looked exhausted, so I got up and gave her my seat, which seemed like the right thing to do. Looking back on it now, I'm surprised I wasn't questioned, lectured, or berated for my actions. I got a lot of dirty looks, but fortunately there was no incident.

It always seemed strange to me that so much was made of the differences between the races. I never really understood or related to societal norms and thought much was lost through this attitude. Around 1954, when I started working, one of my rides to work was with a black gent named Paul who worked at the same temp agency. He was a fine man, a good role model, and a graduate engineer with a wife and a young son aged three or four: a nice family. Paul was also a very talented musician who played piano and had a group that performed at local venues. They played dance and mood music popular at the time. Years later, I found myself at a club outside Boston. As soon as I saw the musicians, I recognized Paul. It was great to reconnect and see him in his true element.

A couple of years later, when I lived at the YMCA in Boston, my roommate was a great guy who happened to be black. He worked with or as a curator at the Museum of Fine Arts. We got along fine. Usually, on Friday nights, there was a well-attended poker game in our room. By the time the stakes got high, I'd usually drop out and fall asleep while the rest of the guys often played through the night. Color had no place in the game.

Our Next Move

At some point I heard my father worked on the Alaska Highway. This project was completed in World War II. I heard later that Dad was responsible for a 50-mile section. The next time I remember seeing Dad, I was around nine years old, and we were on the way to Bolivia. My parents had reunited at some point. I think this was in 1943. In those days we went by air on 21-passenger DC-3s, which flew only during the day. We stayed in a hotel at night. Our destination was Sucre, the old capital. It took about a week to get there. One of the many stops was in La Paz at 12,500 feet. I remember having a Coke, and then passing out. I was put back on the plane with oxygen and recovered.

In Sucre there was no school and I had no contact with other children except my brother. There are seven years between my brother and me. His name is John Gorman Smith, but we called him Gorman. I don't remember any interaction between Gorman and me in the early time there.

We lived in an apartment building that had a large square courtyard in the center. It was two stories with a balcony all around inside with railings on the second floor. There were no windows on the exterior walls of the building, reminiscent of a fortress. It had a large entryway door of heavy wood on the street side with a smaller people door in it: very third world! It was customary for everyone of a certain economic status to have servants who took care of things. They tended to the cleaning, cooking, and even caretaking of my brother, but not of me. I was allowed to roam around by myself. I even went to the movies alone, but I wasn't lonely. I just accepted things as they were. Dad's work was to build a portion of the Pan American Highway. The plan was a road from Alaska to Patagonia. Lots of money was spent, but it was never completed: what a waste!

Our next move was to Cochabamba, still in Bolivia. Our house was in a compound of two houses on about two acres. It was surrounded by a thick wall about ten feet high with broken glass on the top and a big iron gate at the entry. A stream ran through the property. There was a swimming pool where I taught myself to swim. The compound had many trees and landscaping. There was a full-time gardener who lived in a shed on the property. Our residence was located a short distance from the city. Gorman and I slept on army cots, as we did all the time with our parents.

I went to school there and recall I was in fifth grade. The kids at school made it clear I couldn't participate in any of their activities. They hated all Americans. When I tried to break the barrier, things got physical. I accepted my isolation and focused on my teacher who was a very nice lady. She spoke no English and I spoke no Spanish. While communication was difficult, I do remember absorbing and learning things. I particularly remember geometry being one of the subjects covered and how later in life I had a knack for it, which I now believe may have originated there. Other kids I knew from the U.S. went to English language schools in Cochabamba. I don't know how they got there and never gave it a thought at the time. To get to school I rode the public trolley and was completely on my own. Dad had a car and driver. The driver protected the car when Dad wasn't in it. Who protected me? His job provided the car. Reflecting on it now, it strikes me as strange and disheartening that it seemed my value was less than the car Dad didn't own.

CHAPTER 3

Back to the Real World

NEAR THE END OF OUR TIME IN BOLIVIA, WORLD WAR II ended. After Bolivia we returned to Florida via the same old 21-passenger DC-3, again flying only during the day. On the way back, we stayed in a hotel in New Orleans, Louisiana. Much later, we learned my paternal grandfather was the manager. Once in Florida, we stayed at my uncle's, my mother's brother's place. He had a popular restaurant, trailer park, three small rental houses, and a car dealership, all located in Saint Andrews, very near Panama City. He was very wealthy. I remember being taken to the movies by one of the restaurant workers, which was a new experience for me.

We stayed in one of the rental houses, which was actually a log cabin. It was simple and comfortable: two bedrooms, one bath, and a small living room. I don't remember the kitchen. If there was one, we never used it; we ate out for all our meals. The house didn't have a cellar. Uncle Carson had an office and living quarters in the restaurant building. He wasn't married and didn't seem to have a girlfriend.

We lived there for a few months, during which time I went to school. Mom expected I'd have trouble with the schoolwork. She spoke with the teacher, a nice lady, and a first-rate teacher. I don't remember any problem with the schoolwork. I never was a motivated student. I got mostly Bs throughout my school years and even in college.

After living in St. Andrew, we flew to St. Thomas in the Virgin Islands. We lived there for about three years in three different locations. The first was at a marine base that was active at the time. Our neighbors had three boys, and the middle one was about my age. They had a sailboat, and it was there I learned to sail. The beach was close by and I spent a good deal of time there.

Initially I was enrolled in the local Catholic school in St. Thomas, which was standard practice for white families. The other schools had mostly black students. I was in the sixth grade and taught by nuns. I remember there was an incident between my teacher and a student. When Mom heard about it, I was transferred to a non-sectarian private school. I should mention that schools weren't segregated. In my new school, most students were black with only a few whites.

During that year, the marine base closed. I presume it was the reason for our next move. We moved to a compound of three houses. There was no wall, garden, or gardener. It was about halfway between the marine base airport and the town: not the best location. While there, Dad built a rowboat, about 12 feet long, of pine, which was held together with steel screws. This was shortly after the war and other materials weren't available. It leaked terribly. The screws rusted rapidly, and some had to be replaced. Fortunately, it was stolen before it could fall apart. I remember rowing it while Dad fished. I also bailed a lot.

After a short time, we moved to a house on the side of Crown Mountain, the highest point on the island. There was a spectacular view of the harbor and town. It had a garage where Dad built a 14-foot sailboat with a little help from me. Fortunately, I put in some bronze screws this time. He did a great job on it. Unfortunately, Dad was a poor sailor, and I was never allowed to sail it myself.

In St. Thomas it was evident whites were the minority and targeted as such. While we lived there, a local kid who was black, picked a fight with me on the main street. We were evenly matched for size. He was getting beaten badly, and the cops broke it up. The kid was sent home and I went to the police station. Looking back at it, I think it gave me, even in only a small way, a view into the fact that wherever power resides, it's abused.

After I finished sixth grade the only option was public school, so I went there. The teachers were all black and mostly first-rate. During seventh grade, my last year in St. Thomas, there was a student from St. John who came to live with us during the school year. His name was Wally. He was a year older and bigger than me, and a year ahead in school. We got along well. It was a bit of an exchange program, so he spent the school year with us on St. Thomas and I spent the summer on St. John with his family. St. John was located twelve miles from St. Thomas and was a much smaller island.

At the time, John D. Rockefeller owned almost all the island with a few others owning very small areas. St. John was not populated except for a small village at Caneel Bay. The island became a national park much later, I think by gift. It was and is a beautiful place.

Wally's parents remained on St. John. His mother had a drinking problem, and his father was seldom seen: somewhat of a recluse. Supposedly he was carrying out agricultural research. I don't remember ever having a meal with Wally's father present. Hopefully, Wally had more interaction with his father than I did with mine, but I never saw it.

Wally and I swam in a large concrete pool about 100 yards from their large, classic house on the beach. It was the centerpiece of the village of Caneel Bay. We explored the forest nearby but spent most of our time fishing on the reef in a rowboat. In the evening we prepared by scouring the beach for fiddler crabs, which we separated from the shell and used as bait. Once out on the boat, we dunked our faces over the side while wearing sea diving masks to spot the fish below and then dropped a line. Our method was very effective! Every time we went out, we waited until we caught about fifty pounds of fish, then returned to give them to the people in the village. It was an experience I'll never forget.

During our time in St. Thomas, there seemed to be plenty of booze flowing in our house. Rum was bought by the case and always on hand. Interestingly enough, my parents never seemed drunk, thanks to the Creator.

Many, many years later, my parents visited St. Thomas and inquired about Wally's parents. Apparently, so they were told, Wally's dad worked at a bank in the Caribbean and embezzled a large sum of money. He hid on St. John and later killed himself in a hotel in the area. After that, Wally's mom moved to St. Thomas, hooked up with some gigolo, got a sports car, drove off the road, and was killed. The only news about Wally was that he was at the Coast Guard Academy in Connecticut.

CHAPTER 4

Puerto Rico and Albany

NEXT, WE WENT TO SANTURCE, PUERTO RICO, A NEIGH-borhood near San Juan. I think it was 1948. I was in the eighth grade. We lived in a nice neighborhood at two locations. I went to another Catholic school taught by nuns in English. I had some friends in San Juan and in our suburban neighborhood. I don't remember if, or where, my brother went to school.

Since I was the only non-Catholic in my class, I was left alone while my classmates attended services in the church. In the back of the room was a bookcase filled with *Tales of Shakespeare* books, written by Charles and Mary Lamb, that contained most of Shakespeare's plays. These books were written to make the works of Shakespeare understood by children. I think I read them all. One passage from *Hamlet* really impressed me:

> *"... to thine own self be true*
> *And it must follow, as the night the day,*
> *Thou canst not then be false to any man."*

I learned two lessons from this: (1) don't kid yourself or make up stories, and (2) always take responsibility for your actions, don't ever blame others. As I think of it now, I've been guided by this through-out my life. Wow! Shakespeare was quite a guy!

After about a year, we returned to Uncle Carson's place in St. Andrew, Florida. At the time we had a dog, a German Shepherd/mutt mix, named Duke. He was totally bonded to our family. His journey from Puerto Rico with us was eventful. A crate was made for him of wood and chicken wire. I remember as the plane took off in Puerto Rico, we heard him howl over the engine noise. When we landed in Miami and the luggage compartment was opened, he ran out to us. Apparently, he chewed through the chicken wire and escaped. During the layover, the cage was patched, and on the flight to Panama City, he remained inside and seemed adjusted to flying.

After a few summer months at my uncle's place, my parents went on to Albany, New York. Perhaps a week later, I was responsible to get myself, Gorman, and Duke to Albany via more DC-3 flights. I don't remember staying overnight anywhere, but there were multiple flights, and it must have been a long day. Luckily, we arrived as planned.

Of all the places I've lived, Albany was by far the best! I was in ninth grade there. The school was impressive! It was about a half mile long, four stories tall with a five-story administration building in the center, which was made of decorative concrete, while the rest was all brick. The left wing had vocational trades on the first floor. The right wing had gymnasiums on two floors, and an Olympic-size swimming pool. Inside there was a center corridor with classrooms front and back, with at least 30 desks screwed to the floor in each room. It served grades seven through nine.

The teachers were first-rate, and my fellow students were great folks! We lived some distance from the city, about a mile from the airport, so I travelled to school by a long-haul commuter bus, not a school bus. There was one house next door, and the rest of the area was farmland. Although the farmhouses were widely spaced, the community was close-knit. I was invited in and accepted, and I made a good friend nearby. His family had a dairy farm and extensive corn fields. I don't know why, but he didn't attend the same school as I did.

While there I joined the Boy Scouts. There was a swim meet that involved scout troops in Albany. I vividly remember participating in a swim meet that involved five or six troops. Only one other guy in my troop could swim. I let my teammate take first in his event, and I took second. I took first in all the other events except freestyle, where I placed second, but it was close. Our troop placed second overall with only two swimmers! This is the only athletic event my parents attended. Dad's reaction, "Why didn't you pull harder and beat that guy?" I was disappointed he didn't appreciate the magnitude of our second-place finish, mostly due to my contribution. I didn't let Dad's opinion affect me, but instead continued swimming for my school's team where I later earned my letter.

Another thing I loved about Albany was the snow. The road in front of our house had little traffic and a mild slope. I had a pair of skis and practiced on the snow-covered road. It was here my love of skiing began.

CHAPTER 5

Stoughton High School Years

IN 1949, AFTER ABOUT SIX MONTHS IN ALBANY, DAD WAS transferred to the Boston, Massachusetts office. Our residence was located in Stoughton, within commuting distance to Boston.

We drove from Albany to Stoughton, which in those days was a two-day trip. We stayed in a hotel in Framingham on the way.

Our new home was in a large development of mostly identical houses on small lots. There were hundreds of rental houses, which made it easy to get lost the first time in there. I think the development was built as housing for workers in the town's factories during World War II. It was called Pine Crest Acres.

Most of the residents were "blue collar," but there were a significant number who seemed to be professional folks as well. My impression was that the professional folks were saving to buy a house. Those I knew had no kids.

Our house was small. There were three bedrooms, two of which could accommodate two beds. In the third bedroom, one bed fit in a "notch" so small that access was limited to a narrow area about three feet wide. (In my present house I have a walk-in closet the same size). There was a full bath with shower, a living room, and a kitchen large enough to accommodate a small table. The house sat on a concrete slab and had no cellar. There was a tiny utility room for the oil furnace. The oil tank was outside, which is certainly unusual nowadays.

A funny incident occurred during the time we lived in Pine Crest Acres. In those days, deliveries were left in the house when no one was home. Doors were seldom locked. One time the dry cleaning was delivered and left in the living room. When the delivery man started to go, our large dog, Duke, wouldn't allow him to leave. The poor guy was stuck in the house for about an hour until we got home.

We lived there for about three years. After that, my parents bought a modest ranch house in town. I was in the last half of ninth grade, so I went to Stoughton High School. Of all the places I lived and schools I attended, Stoughton was the worst. It was an old school, built in 1923. The class schedules were on double sessions: grades eleven and twelve in the morning, grades nine and ten in the afternoon. The teachers were mostly poor educators, with only a few good ones. There was no gym or auditorium.

Stoughton was a mill town. My fellow students were a rough bunch. For the first month or so I was harassed, and a number of students tried to pick fights. Finally, I picked one with the school bully who was a year older and 20 pounds heavier. In those days, fights had rules: fists only, no kicking or hitting below the belt. These were strict boxing rules, which were honored by everyone. We went at it in the boy's room between classes. It was a draw. After that, my opponent never bothered me again. There were a few others who picked fights, but I won easily and was finally left in peace.

I had no trouble with the schoolwork, but I had a sour attitude towards the town. Fortunately, I found a good friend, a new student from Canada named Alan. As far as academic work was concerned, we were equal. We studied together and compared notes. No one bothered him, perhaps because we were friends.

My Finest Mentor

Early in my time in Stoughton, I met the finest man I've ever known. His name was Leo Estabrook. He was my mentor and role model. He also was my safety net, a role usually filled by parents. We shared the hobby of model airplanes, which was a popular hobby at the time for teens and adults.

There were many contests in our area with rules for all events and classes for both gas engine and rubber band planes. For gas engine powered planes, the size of the engines determined the class. Leo and I built kits, commercial offerings as well as designs featured in magazines. Neither of us did well in competition, so I started to develop my own designs.

There were lots of crashes! I subscribed to a magazine that had good technical articles on aircraft design. One of the articles described wingtip turbulence, which caused lots of drag and reduced lift. To me, the solution seemed simple: (1) duplicate the airfoil section, but make it larger, and (2) overhang the top, bottom, front, and back. I called them "wing dams." In contests using my design, I usually placed first but never less than second. My design didn't look like any of the other designs at that time; all features were strictly functional. In newer commercial airliners, you'll see similar devices to my wing dam design.

I don't remember how I came to know Leo. I think it was another case of divine guidance. Leo had a greater impact on my life than any other adult, even more than my parents. In fact, I think he saved my life! He was my island of sanity in a sea of chaos.

He was about eight years older than me and a very pragmatic person. His morals and ethics met the highest standard, and he was the hardest working person I ever met. We spent a lot of time together. How he found time to enjoy our shared hobby, and do all he did, is one of life's mysteries.

When we met, Leo, his wife Helen, and three-year-old son Donald lived in an apartment. Leo's direct family was in Canada, or so I understood. He had a cousin, who looked more like his brother, who was an actor in Hollywood and had many supporting roles in the movies.

In World War II, Leo was stationed in Wendover, Nevada. He trained to be a tail gunner on B-29s, the plane that dropped the atomic bombs on Japan. Fortunately, the war ended and he never saw combat.

Leo was very close to Helen's family. When we first met, I thought her family lived in poverty, despite the fact they all worked. Hers was a large family of six or seven kids. I think she was the second youngest. She had a younger brother named Burton, about my age. He went to Boston Trade School, and we became good friends.

Helen's father passed away early in our relationship. Leo took over as de-facto family head.

Helen's mother, Mom Cushing, was a great lady, loved by all who knew her. In spite of the family's economic struggles, she was one of the most giving persons I ever met. She had physical limitations and seldom left the apartment.

About a year after I met him, Leo bought a large house in Stoughton. It had three stories and a detached two-car garage. The top floor was unfinished. He did extensive renovations and made an apartment on the third floor. The first floor was rented, and the second floor was for Mom Cushing, who everybody called "Mom," and Burton. The rest of Helen's family had moved on.

Leo worked as an auto body repair man and was a true artist at his trade. He could pound out dents and paint a car so expertly that you never knew anything happened. To make extra money, Leo bought late model cars with low mileage that were a total loss by insurance, then restored them for resale. He also had a sound system he operated for weddings and similar celebrations.

After I graduated from high school, and was working, I didn't see Leo much. After Franny and I got married, it was even less. By the time all our kids were in school, I learned Leo developed liver cancer. The cause was acetone exposure from the bodywork painting. He was about 60 years old when he passed away and is one of those whom I miss the most.

We stayed in contact with Mom Cushing for many years. She lived in subsidized housing in Stoughton. We took her out to lunch and to our house in Attleboro. I'm not sure when Mom Cushing passed away.

Helen moved to Florida but spent Christmas with her family up here. We saw her only once when she visited us in Wareham. I always expressed my gratitude for their help in my teen years. As far as I know, Helen is still in Florida. I heard by letters that she was in very bad shape. I'm so grateful for the wonderful gift of Leo and Helen's efforts in my formative years.

Keeping Busy

Throughout my four years in high school, I held several jobs to support my activities. I worked at a chicken farm and as an usher at the local theater. I had other jobs at different times, including employment at a grocery store, a shoe factory, and performing various jobs for neighbors.

While in high school, at about age 16 or 17, my parents went on vacation. This happened twice, during which time I took care of Gorman while they were away. By this time, he didn't need a sitter, just meals and such. It was summer and there was no school. For most families that would mean a family vacation, but not for us.

Some of my best memories during high school are of skiing at Blue Hills. This ski area was located in Canton, a neighboring town, not far away. In those days there seemed to be plenty of snow. I skied there for several years before one of the lift attendants noticed I didn't have a ticket to indicate I had paid. Oops! I always assumed it was free.

In high school I was on the track team. I ran the mile, the half mile, and the quarter mile. Since I didn't smoke, I was the only one who could do it. My many part-time jobs took up my spare time, so I never trained. Because the coach had no other options, he went along with it. Unfortunately, my limited efforts weren't enough, and I usually lost in competition

Aside from sports, I certainly had an interest in girls. I dated none from Stoughton, but a number from surrounding towns. I remember one situation when I worked as an usher. There was a girl with a group from out of town. She was pretty, well-developed, and expressed an interest in me. She tried to set up a date in her home. At that time, I was about 16. She indicated she was 13. I was flattered but told her I thought the age difference was too great. I don't recall how I handled it, but apparently, we parted as friends. Her name was Kathy.

Two years after our meeting, I got a phone call from Kathy. This started a three-year relationship. For me, it was serious, and I thought we would marry when we were ready. Kathy agreed. She lived in Sharon, the next town about five miles away. I had no car, so I hitchhiked or walked to get there. On one of my walks, I was stopped by a cop from her town and treated roughly. I talked to Kathy's parents about it, and her dad suggested I make a complaint, which I did. That later came back to haunt me.

I had a good relationship with her family and was included in their activities. This included dinner every Saturday evening. They had a very large, fancy house, which was not surprising since her father owned an advertising agency. Sharon was an upscale town, a residential, very affluent community, whereas Stoughton was a factory town.

Regardless of where we lived, whenever one was available, Dad joined the local country club. He was an excellent golfer, always shooting in the 60s and 70s on 18-hole courses. I used to caddy for him on occasion. Dad had many lucky shots that crushed the dreams of his opponents.

Mom was mostly sober upon moving to Stoughton, but within a year or so, she was mostly drunk. As time went on, she was virtually never sober. Dad was sober during the week and drunk on weekends, sometimes to the point he couldn't stand. At that point, Dad started to beat Mom on weekends. This happened every weekend. My brother called it "Saturday Night Fights!"

CHAPTER 6

The End of Saturday Night Fights

AT ABOUT AGE 18, I HAD ENOUGH OF THE SATURDAY Night Fights. One time, it must have started on Friday. As Dad started, I got between them and demanded Dad stop. He said he'd take care of me and came at me. I snapped! I don't remember what I did, but I think I would've killed him if Mom hadn't pulled me off. Mom grabbed me and yelled, "Stop! You're going to kill him!" During the altercation, Gorman never left our bedroom and there was no conversation between us. When it was over, Dad kicked me out of the house and spent the next two weeks in bed.

The fact I snapped was scary. I realized in that state I was dangerous. It was a pivotal moment in my life. I can say I resolved to never be out of control like that again, and to this day I think I've kept this resolution.

After the incident, I walked five miles to my girlfriend Kathy's and her family put me up for the weekend. When Monday arrived, I had to go back to school.

Leo put me up for a week and a half and I never missed a day of school. Leo's comment was, "How did you come out of that crazy place in one piece?"

After my time at Leo's, I was called back home and told I could stay. I told Dad, "If that ever happens again, it will happen again." To this he agreed. At least when I was there, there were no more incidents. Much later, I wondered if Dad wanted me back to help ensure the keeper of his darkest secret was close by. Clearly news of him being known as a wife beater could end his career. The way I felt about it was rather neutral at that time. As they say, "Blood is thicker than water." While I felt some kind of connection to him, it became clear later that it wasn't the same for Dad.

CHAPTER 7

The Breakup and Employment

A FTER GRADUATION FROM HIGH SCHOOL IN 1953, I needed a full-time job. Our next-door neighbor, Jim, noted my success with model airplanes. He was Sales Manager for an engineering temp agency in Boston. I was hired as a tracer. In those days, engineering drawings were drawn by hand on paper. Duplicating them caused the drawings to literally wear out, so they had to be duplicated by tracing. I was very fast and accurate on the drawing board and really enjoyed the work. Getting to work was very difficult, if not impossible, without a car, which I didn't have. So, I got a ride from two men who lived in the area and also worked there.

During this time, I thought it might be smart to pursue the option of going to college, whether part- or full-time. Financially I knew I needed assistance. I asked Dad if he could help me out and he said, "Do it yourself." That ended that possibility, so I stayed on my current path.

After I accumulated a few dollars, I bought a used car, a Nash sedan, so I was able to get around. One night, I drove Kathy to her babysitting job. The parents of the kids she was minding were going to drive her home. On my way home, there was a sharp corner, followed by a steep hill. The pavement on the hill was covered with loose gravel. As the car tires hit the gravel, the road curved to the right and the car went straight, heading off the road. It slid down the hill, went off the edge of the road and hit a road sign, which stopped the car. Even though there were no seat belts in those days, I was not un-seated, but the bumper was bent back to the tire in front, so the car was not drivable. Somehow a cop showed up. Unfortunately, it was the one I complained about. The next thing I knew I was charged with "driving to endanger," or so I was told.

I consulted Dad about it. That was a big mistake! He recommended a golfing buddy as my lawyer. Shortly thereafter, my lawyer and I drove the same route as I had and nearly duplicated my accident. A hearing was scheduled, and I was off to the next step.

The hearing was held somewhere in Boston. Those present were my father, my lawyer, the cop I complained about, and the judge, whom I didn't know. The judge was casually dressed without a formal black robe. The room was bare except for a lectern, like you would see at a wake, and a few folding chairs. There was no raised dais. Mine was the only case heard. I felt like a lamb going to the slaughter. The hearing was very brief. The cop acted as the prosecutor and the judge pronounced the sentence—I was to lose my license, never to be allowed to drive in Massachusetts again. No one else said one word, not even my lawyer. Wow! I paid my lawyer $265.00. In today's money that would be about $3,000.00. I accepted the sentence and moved into the YMCA in Boston.

I was still dating Kathy and there was a commuter train that went to Sharon where she still lived with her parents. The train station was a short walk to her house. Kathy had started college and we saw each other once a week. One Saturday night as I was on my way out after dinner, she reminded me of my failings and dumped me. My last words to her were, "You'll never find anyone who will love you as much as I do." With that, I walked away. In retrospect, I've wondered if my driving conviction influenced Kathy's decision.

How did I feel after being dumped? I was crushed, of course, but I never felt anger or thoughts of revenge. Being the pragmatist that I am, I knew that in a long relationship it has to work for both parties. If it doesn't work for one, it won't work for either. So, I wished her well and hoped she'd find a partner with whom to have a happy life. I didn't think much about it at the time. I tried to put it out of my mind and move on.

Love is the most powerful of all the emotions. I can't imagine I could ever harm or even wish harm to one I love. This is how I felt then, which is the same as I feel now.

A little less than a year later, I was walking somewhere when I was approached by a Boston cop in uniform whom I didn't know. He said, "I've investigated your case. There was a miscarriage of justice. I set it right. You can now go get your license." I don't know where this came from, but I was very grateful.

Only recently did I stop to analyze the series of events and wonder about their legitimacy. Did this really happen? Was Dad's golfing buddy really a lawyer? Was I actually in a courtroom? Did Dad somehow orchestrate the entire process? Until now, I never questioned it, but as I write this, I wonder what would've happened if I'd been more observant, questioned the proceedings, or not accepted the sentence. What did I know as a 19- or 20-year-old?

It's clear now that these events set me on a path that led to greater joy in my life: another example of divine guidance!

CHAPTER 8

Moseley's, Work, and Gorman

I GAVE A LOT OF THOUGHT TO THE BREAKUP. I WAS CRUSHED but only looked to the future. First, there was my behavior. I recognized I could be more considerate and thoughtful of others. Second, I considered what specifications a person must have to be my ideal partner for the rest of my life. It was a long, detailed list, but the short version is:

1. Non-smoker
2. Intelligent
3. Independent
4. Compatible
5. Perceptive
6. Logical
7. Trustworthy

Had I not been dumped, I never would've thought of this. To find this person, I had a number of options now that I had wheels. I never smoked and my drinking was limited to a few glasses of wine, or a beer in social situations. My lifestyle was, and is, very moderate and I wanted someone similar. I wondered where I might be most likely to find a compatible partner.

I chose ballrooms as my preferred venues. My favorite was Moseley's on the Charles in Dedham. It was quite formal there, as in all ballrooms. Girls generally wore cocktail dresses or Sunday best and high heels, but they also allowed work attire: skirt, blouse, and penny loafers. Only a few girls came dressed that way. For guys, it was a suit or jacket with dress pants, a white shirt, tie, and leather shoes.

In those days, the music was loud enough to dance to, but not so loud that you couldn't have a conversation. My routine in going to ballrooms was to get there early and check out the girls as they came in. I'd pick the best looking one and see how it went. I met a lot of nice girls in the two years of my search, but none met the specs.

I've always thought of myself as a gentleman and tried to act accordingly. At one point during my trips to Moseley's, I met a very lovely girl named Carol. She was exceptionally beautiful, fun, and good company. We went on a number of dates. When I had no plans, I'd call her. She was always available. One time she said, "Oh, sorry, I have a date." I said, "Okay, perhaps another time," to which she replied, "Oh, I'll cancel. I'd rather go out with you." Most guys wouldn't have hesitated. What was my reaction? I really felt bad. What had I done? I knew she didn't meet the specs. While I enjoyed her company, we weren't able to hold conversations at the level I desired. Until that moment, I hadn't realized I was leading her on in a relationship that was going nowhere, and, in the process, she could be badly hurt. I still feel a little guilty about this. I begged off and never saw her again. She was so nice. I'm sure she found a good partner and a happy life.

During this time, my work situation had undergone a number of changes. When I started in Boston, I made $1.00 an hour, which was minimum wage. Within six months, I progressed from tracer to detailer. Others in that job got around $2.00. I asked for a raise and was refused. I looked elsewhere and found a job paying $1.75, so I gave notice. When my employer matched it, I decided to stay. The way things were organized, the designer did the overall design, then the detailer did drawings of the individual parts. At that time, this work was for tools, fixtures, and such to make parts for mass production. In another six months, I was a designer, with a detailer who made more than I did. I again asked for a raise and was refused. I went looking and was offered around $2.50. Again, they wanted to match it, but this time I decided to leave.

The neighbor who got me the job said, "Why you S.O.B.! We brought you in and taught you everything you know. If I ever get a chance to screw you, I will."

After that, I made a number of job changes. The second to last temp company I worked for was in Worcester, closer to the ski areas. For years, I'd always been able to find others with whom to ski, but now from the office in Worcester, there were more opportunities.

Around that time, I remember my mother saying to me, "Take care of your brother," so I bought the necessary clothing and equipment and took him on some weekend ski trips. He took to it rather quickly and became a pretty good skier.

At one point, the temp agency offered me a position in Springfield, Vermont. I spent a winter there skiing every weekend and then some. While in Springfield, I met Roger Smith who became a lifelong friend.

Outside of ski season, or when the skiing was poor, I was off to the ballrooms. There were lots of nice girls, but they weren't meeting the specs. How could I get away with being so fussy?

During that time, Gorman got into lots of trouble. Mom told me they spent thousands of dollars keeping him out of jail. I vividly remember her saying, "Gorman will tell a lie when the truth will do better." In my opinion, this remained true certainly during the time we had a relationship. Clearly being born into chaos and not having the advantage of a stable early life had an effect on his development.

Gorman was kicked out of school and never made it into ninth grade. I remember bailing him out of trouble once. He was holed up in a friend's house in Stoughton and called me to come save him. There were two guys waiting in a car for him to come out. They burned a leather jacket I bought for him. It was hanging on the electrical wires between two poles, still burning. The story was that one of the guys had a girlfriend whom Gorman was also dating. That guy had just been released from jail and wanted to eliminate the competition. When I arrived, I picked up a piece of pipe I had in my car and approached the other car. I asked what they were doing there. The driver replied, "Nothing." I strongly suggested, while holding the pipe, that they leave. This ended the crisis. Gorman was never bothered after that.

Many months later, an incident happened at home that showed how I fit in the family. At high school graduation, I was given a class ring. Although it was very nice, I didn't wear it much. It had been in my jewelry box, but I noticed it was missing. I asked Mom about it. She said, "I gave it to your brother because he didn't have one, and since we paid for it, it was my choice." That told me all I needed to know. After that, I didn't stay with my parents much.

Our mother planned all this. I learned much later, in a conversation with Gorman's first wife, Gail, that she didn't know Gorman never made it into ninth grade and was very surprised. When he gave her the class ring, she assumed he was a high school graduate. If her parents thought he wasn't, there wouldn't have been a wedding. Years later in 1960, she lost the ring while horseback riding. Clearly, my mom's efforts resulted in many unhappy, messed up lives.

How do I feel about the ring debacle? I didn't think about it then. As I consider it now, it seems my parents wanted my life to be a failure. I thank the Creator and my divine guide that this wasn't the case. I hope my parents were disappointed.

PART TWO

MY LIFE BEGINS

1957—Vaughn and Franny

CHAPTER 9

A New Beginning

MY LIFE TRULY BEGAN WHEN I MET FRANNY. OF ALL the stories of my life, there's one that happened against all odds. Four events led to our meeting. Had these not happened in exactly the sequence and timing they did, we would never have met. Franny became the love of my life, wife, partner, and best friend. This could be nothing else but an example of divine guidance.

Meeting Franny

One day I was washing my car in my parents' driveway. The house was on a main road to Kathy's town. She happened by and stopped at the end of the driveway. She called me over and attempted a conversation. For me, it was too emotional. I couldn't respond properly. After a few awkward moments, she left.

A few weeks later, I got a call from Kathy's mother. This was two years after I was dumped. I think it was 1957. She asked me to come to their house. When I got there, Kathy's mother and I had a conversation. She invited me to dinner that Saturday and I accepted. As I finished dressing in preparation to go there, I realized I didn't want to get involved again. Instead, I decided to go to Moseley's.

I arrived late and all the well-dressed girls were taken. All who were left were those dressed for work. Of the six or eight, one was taller than the others. I asked her to dance and found we had interests in common. Her name was Frances Mullin. Franny planned to go to Moseley's with her girlfriend that same evening. The friend canceled and Franny would've normally stayed home, but this time she didn't! And so, my life began!!

Somehow, I sensed Franny was special. It wasn't that she was exceptionally beautiful. At that time, I thought I'd gone out with girls who were more physically attractive, but she was very intelligent. At some point I realized what a woman has between her ears is far more interesting than the physical part. That night we went out for coffee at Dunkin' Donuts. She had her own car, which was very unusual for girls in those days. I got her number and called her for a date the following week. She begged off. There was a holiday and she wanted to spend it with her family. I thought she was rejecting me until she said, "How about next week?" Wow, that was close!

After that, we became a steady thing. The first kiss didn't come until after the sixth date: slow going, so I didn't spook her.

Her interests exposed me to things I hadn't done before. We went to plays, Symphony Hall concerts, and other similar things. In good weather, she introduced me to water skiing. I got a small boat with a 70 HP motor which was very big at the time. I became a good water skier and we enjoyed lots of fun on the water.

As I got to know Franny better, I realized she was meeting all the specs!

The Bonding Incident

There was one incident when we were going together that I think established the strong bond and commitment between us. We were "steadies" for about six months. At that time, there was a party at the place I worked. I asked Franny to go with me, but she declined. She said, "I don't want to be on display." I wanted to go, so I called one of my past girlfriends. To cover my tracks with Franny, I invented the story that I had a National Guard meeting. This occurred before, so I thought it was believable. As it happened, we never made it to the party.

The next time I spoke to Franny, she asked many questions. I thought I answered them well, until she said, "That must have been a real challenge in the dark." Over the course of further conversation, I learned that on the night in question she drove to the National Guard facility and noted the lights were out. Wow! I was busted! Then she said, "I don't own you, and I can't tell you what to do, but don't you ever lie to me."

To many guys this would've been a put down. To me, it showed she cared, perhaps to the point of making a decision about our future relationship. It confirmed she was a solid, absolutely reliable person, perhaps the best one with whom to share my life.

About Franny

Franny came from a large, loving family. She had six siblings, three brothers and three sisters. Franny was the sixth child. The oldest were twin girls who were very active in the family structure.

In school, Franny was a serious student. By age eight she knew she wanted to be a teacher. She was focused on preparation and committed to her studies. She graduated from Boston Teachers' College in 1953: the only one in her family with a four-year degree. When we met, Franny had been teaching for two years at a small school in Weymouth where she taught second grade.

The Mullin Family was fairly well off. Her father, Joseph Mullin, was an executive for a company in the textile business. Franny was her father's favorite. A short exposure to the family was all that was needed to see this. I was puzzled that none of her siblings seemed to notice or care. I asked one of the twins about it and she said, "Yeah, everybody knows that." The fact that it didn't seem to bother anyone, and everyone got along so well, showed me the family was a very happy one.

Franny's parents were interesting. Her mother, Frances Sibertz, was pure first-generation German. Her dad was second-generation pure Irish. Although she didn't resemble either parent, I think she favored the German side. All her siblings looked more Irish. Franny's hair was brown except in the summer when it became blonde. She was taller than most girls at that time, around 5 feet 7 inches. When we met, she said she weighed 160 pounds, but looked like 130. She had a tiny 24-inch waist and elegant proportions she tried to hide with her clothing selections. She was a pretty girl who got more lovely as she got older.

Franny was very intelligent and knew her own mind. She was a deeply religious Catholic. I remember a discussion we had early on during which I reminded her of some bad actions by the church. Her position was that some administrators in the church were responsible; it wasn't the religion itself. Wow, one can't argue with that!

We had many discussions as we got to know each other. We respected each other's point of view and were completely open with our views.

When we met, her dad was basically retired, but had a rather menial job as a manual worker in a chocolate factory. I think he did this to avoid being bored. He was a great guy, one of those folks I miss. He had a great, very dry, sense of humor. At our wedding, he went up to a group from the Smith side, took out his hanky, wiped his brow and said, "We had a hell of a time getting rid of her!" The story made rounds long after the event. This was typical Mr. M. He got the exact reaction he wanted.

I think because Franny was his favorite child, and perhaps the way I treated her, I became the favorite son-in-law. Mr. M and I became great friends.

Franny's mother suffered from agoraphobia. She was very uncomfortable in public or in the presence of folks she didn't know. She was very hard to get to know. After a long time, my presence was finally accepted.

Franny tended to be very modest and was a bit shy in new social situations. She had a good, very dry sense of humor, as well as many, many, witty expressions. There was always something new she would come up with or a way to phrase things that were unique to her. To encourage the kids to be efficient and not take their time with tasks, she'd tell them to not do so "a chocolate chip at a time." There was "no horrid talk" at the dinner table, but she always encouraged and enjoyed jocularity. One had to get to know her to see all of this. She was intelligent, wise, and witty. Wow, I was blessed she chose me!

In 1957, the Korean War was in full swing. A few months before I met Franny, I joined the National Guard to avoid being drafted for two years. It was a three-year commitment that required three months active duty for training. While waiting for the training to be assigned, I attended weekly meetings, monthly gatherings, and two weeks of training during the summer. During that time, my relationship with Franny became more serious and we both wanted to make sure I completed my active-duty training before our married life together began. Near the end of my first year in the Guard, I was sent to Fort Sam Houston in San Antonio, Texas for my active-duty training as a medic.

When I returned home three months later, there was no longer work at the engineering temp agency in Worcester. I found a similar drafting job in Waltham. The guy who got me started in the business was a big gun there. He still had hard feelings about what happened years ago, so when he heard I was there, I was fired.

In the course of my job search, I ran into a man who remembered me from somewhere we both worked before. To this day, I have no recollection of the man or our previous connection. He suggested I go to Standard Fittings, located in Framingham, and apply. I did and was hired. The company made high pressure fittings used in the atomic plants being built at the time. The owner also had other companies. One made machinery for recycling plastics, and another had a government contract for gun sights for tanks. I worked on all of it!

The owner was a really decent guy and made it a point to hire all types of individuals. One of the guys who worked for and with me was deaf. Luckily for me, he was incredibly good at reading lips. After a while of working together, we reached a point where we both understood each other well enough so communication wasn't an issue. He was a good draftsman, and we became friends, each learning from one another. He finally left for a better job, and I wished him well. The circumstances that brought me to this job seemed like misfortune but turned out to be an improvement for everyone involved: another case of divine guidance.

CHAPTER 10

Marriage and Settling Down

WHILE I WORKED IN FRAMINGHAM, FRANNY AND I got married. The date was February 14, 1959, Valentine's Day. Since Franny was her father's favorite child, I got the feeling no expense was spared for this event. In preparation for our wedding, I spent some time with the priest. While at first Franny hoped I'd convert to Catholicism, I knew I wasn't comfortable making that type of commitment unless it felt true, which it didn't. Instead, I had to sign and swear I wouldn't interfere with Franny's practice of her religion, and our children would be raised Catholic. That was fine with me. With that completed, I thought we'd receive the church's blessing we deserved. What I didn't expect was, since I didn't convert, I wasn't seen as a member of their community. That was evident when our vows took place outside the altar railing rather than inside, which would've been the case if we were both Catholic. If I had a firm belief system and felt strongly there may have been a conflict, but I accepted the rules knowing it was more important to me that Franny was comfortable and happy above all else.

Franny was a beautiful bride. Her gown was very modest; it even had long sleeves. It was made of delustered satin and showed off her figure, emphasizing her tiny waist and all the rest.

Her three sisters and two close friends were her bridesmaids. Priscilla and Patricia, her two older twin sisters, made all the dresses from a large bolt of burgundy velvet. The result was a beautiful gown fitted to the waist with a flowing skirt below the knee. The results certainly looked professional.

Gorman was my best man. The groomsmen were Franny's three brothers and my buddy from high school, Alan McLean.

After the ceremony at Sacred Heart Parish in Roslindale, we went to a banquet hall in Weymouth for the reception. There were about 100 guests present, most from Franny's side. There were lots of flowers, the majority of which were beautiful burgundy tinted lilies. Throughout the rest of my life I never saw flowers like that again.

It was a very formal affair. Weddings are all about the bride. I must admit it was a bit of a blur for me. I can't remember anything about the band or even the menu, but I did enjoy it. Thanks to the generosity of Mr. M, it was a great way to start our life together.

Prior to the wedding, we decided to make housing arrangements, so we'd have a place all set to live after we got married. We wanted our home to be convenient for both of us. We got a map and looked for the spot an equal distance from both Weymouth and Framingham. The spot was Canton. We found an apartment located in what was the old Canton Poor Farm. The rent was $55.00 a month. The main structure had seven apartments, and there was a small pond on the property that served as a source of ice in the old days. It was interesting to me that the old icehouse and ramp still stood alongside. During our time there, the property owner stocked the pond with trout.

For our honeymoon, we spent a week in Vermont skiing. Franny preferred to stay close to home and didn't want to go anywhere far. While dating we skied a couple of times together. She seemed to enjoy it and I liked that she enjoyed one of my passions. Spending time together up north as a newlywed couple sounded like a great plan. We tried various ski areas in Vermont. I knew the key to happiness would be to help her take it slow and progress gradually. Most places we went worked out well. One of my favorites was Big Bromley in Manchester, Vermont. It had a beginner's trail called Lord's Prayer; the name alone sounded good to Franny. The trails at Bromley were well groomed, which was unusual at the time. One resort I wanted to try was Mad River Glen in Waitsfield because it just opened a new beginner area called the New and Gentle Grasshopper. It was a single chair lift with little-to-no trail grooming. As we approached the ski lift, I asked the lift operator, "Where is the New and Gentle Grasshopper?" To my surprise the guy pointed up to a rather steep, wide-open area, much steeper than you'd expect for beginners. Franny and I used the J-bar lift to visit the Grasshopper. It was far from gentle. Making sudden sharp turns is difficult for beginners and making them on a steep incline is even worse. The Grasshopper's many switchbacks didn't result in much fun for Franny. She tried a couple of runs, then gave up: not our best day. We ended our week on a high at Killington Ski Area, which had opened in December 1958. Nowadays it's one of the biggest, most elaborate ski resorts in Vermont. Back then it was quite small with only three poma lifts and no chair lifts. We both thoroughly enjoyed our time there. It was a fun week; one I'll never forget.

Back at home, we tried to live on what I made and save Franny's salary. Once our family began, she stopped working. Although early in our married life we decided Franny and I would jointly manage our finances, after a short time I realized she could handle this better alone. There was one checking account into which I deposited my paycheck. If I needed money, I asked Franny Girl. She did an amazing job managing it all.

One day after I got home from work, I noticed Franny seemed upset about something. I didn't pursue the matter as I figured she'd inform me when she was ready. After a time, Franny confessed what she thought was her great sin about which I'd be disappointed and angry. As I sat on the couch, she approached in an agitated state and confessed, "I was overdrawn on the checking account." My immediate reaction was one I don't think she expected. I replied, "I'm glad you're managing the account. I'm sure if it was me, the problem would've been worse!" At first Franny seemed upset that I didn't react the way she thought I would. It took a minute or two for her to process that I wasn't upset, and she was relieved. I hope it was one of those times she realized I trusted her implicitly and would always be on her side.

We lived in Canton for about a year and a half. During this time our first child was born, Clement V. Smith IV. We called him Clemmy. He arrived in October 1959, about a month early and a little underweight, but otherwise seemingly healthy. Clemmy was the center of Franny's universe, as most babies are for their mothers. Franny thoroughly enjoyed motherhood and was a very devoted mother. She was always truly his guiding light.

When Clemmy was three months old, Franny became pregnant with our second child. Our family was growing and life was good. One day when Clemmy was about six months old, Franny took him to a well-baby clinic appointment. The doctors found he had a heart problem. Shortly thereafter, Franny and her father took Clemmy to Boston Children's Hospital where he spent several days for evaluation. Many tests were performed, including a heart catheterization. In addition to determining he had a ventricular septal defect, or hole between two of the chambers in his heart, they also discovered he was mentally handicapped, which was termed "retarded" in those days; now it's considered to be offensive. Although there weren't many details, they said it was probably brain damage. We were told they weren't quite sure of the seriousness of his mental deficits, and we should bring him back at the age of four for further evaluation. Clemmy was prescribed medications for his heart. Franny's reaction to all of this? "I know how to handle this. I've had the training!" Little did I know that her teaching education included special education training.

Looking back, upon learning of Clemmy's condition, there was no panic or fear. We both accepted the situation and considered it a challenge we'd meet. There was no disagreement on this. I followed Franny's lead and backed her up in all ways I could. She almost always had the best course of action for family problems.

In 1960, my contract with the National Guard came up for renewal. Since the Korean War was still going on, I felt the need to re-enlist so I could stay state-side. Rather than continuing with the National Guard, where I'd have to commute to Boston, I decided to enlist with the Army Reserve as an army medic at a field hospital unit in Taunton for another three-year term.

In September 1960, Mary Elizabeth Smith was born. At first, Clemmy didn't seem to notice her arrival. Mary, like Clemmy, was an excellent baby. She'd wake up maybe once during the night to feed and then return to sleep easily. I remember all our children being really good babies.

Shortly after Mary arrived, we moved to our house at 8 Merigan Way in Foxboro. Franny provided the down payment from her teachers' retirement fund. Our house was a small Cape on a dead-end street of perhaps 20 similar houses, which was ideal for kids.

I remember early on when Mary was learning to talk and her attempts to refer to Clemmy as her brother came out as "Buzzy." It stuck as his nickname for many, many years until his early twenties, when he no longer liked it, and we reverted back to Clemmy.

In November 1960, Gorman and his wife, Gail, moved in with us. They eloped to New Hampshire that August, then had a church wedding at St. Mary's Catholic Church in Foxboro. Shortly thereafter they came to live in our unfinished attic for a short time before renting a house on the other side of town. While there, they started their family. Although we had families and lived in the same town, we didn't get together often. On most Saturdays, when I went to the dump, I'd stop by for a quick visit, but that was the extent of it.

Gorman was very different from me. Because he had so little

education, or interest in learning, his options were limited. The one thing he did have was great artistic talent. After getting married, thanks to his father-in-law, he got a job as an illustrator for a shoe catalog. In December 1961, Gorman and Gail had their first child, John.

In March 1962, Grace Rebecca Smith, our third child was born. She was named after my mother. In her early years, she expressed her dislike of the name Grace and asked to be called Becky, a shortened version of her middle name. Franny was now extremely busy with three children under the age of three.

Around that time, we learned there was a parents' group in the neighboring town of Attleboro for families of children with developmental disabilities. There were also Catholic schools for all grades; Attleboro had a lot to offer. We became very active in the parents' group. The group had two activities they funded: a nursery school and a summer camp. The name of the group was "The Attleboro Area Association for Retarded Citizens," or ARC for short. I realize "retarded" is not used these days to describe those who are mentally handicapped, but I included it here because it was used then. I ran the fundraising drive in Foxboro for a few years and was surprised I was good at it. After that, I persuaded the local Ford dealer, Rodman Ford, to take the reins and he ran it for many years. I also served one term as President.

The experience with fundraising and being President was a great confidence builder for me. It served me well in my later years in my career. Clemmy indirectly was responsible for this and has my gratitude. Another case of divine guidance?

CHAPTER 11

Attleboro and Gorman's Divorce

I N NOVEMBER 1964, OUR FOURTH CHILD ARRIVED. WE
didn't have a name picked out in advance, and I remember having
a conversation with Mr. M months before during which I joked
that I just couldn't see naming the child Joe Smith; that was way too
generic. But when the baby arrived on Mr. M's birthday, there was
no question he'd be named Joseph James.

By 1966, our little house became too small. It was either enlarge
it or move. We decided to move and put the Foxboro house on the
market. While considering the surrounding cities and towns, Attleboro stuck out from the rest for many reasons, including the fact
there were Catholic schools for the kids, and a school with programs well-suited to Clemmy's needs, which was run by nuns. One
day, Roger Smith was visiting, heard about our anticipated move,
and expressed interest in purchasing our home. Before anyone else
looked at our house, we made a deal with Roger. He lived there until
he passed away in 2021.

We found a raised ranch in Attleboro at 15 Nathaniel Paine
Road that met our needs. My commute was longer, about 20 miles,
but it was worth it.

Shortly after our move, Gorman divorced Gail and moved in with us. He was required to pay child support, but never did. He justified it by saying Gail would simply waste the money and the kids wouldn't benefit from it, so he had no intention of meeting his responsibilities.

One day while I was at work, Franny received a phone call from a Ford dealership letting her know "Mr. Smith's new Mustang is ready to be picked up." Franny told the salesman he must be mistaken, but he insisted, so she told him she'd talk to me and call him back. She just couldn't believe I'd do such a thing. Franny called me at work (something she'd normally never do), so I knew it must be important. Immediately upon hearing about the situation, I knew it had to be Gorman. I told her we'd deal with it after work.

Later that day, Gorman rolled up to the house in his brand-new Mustang. At this point, we reached our limit with Gorman not making child support payments and disregarding his responsibilities, so we kicked him out.

During the time of the separation and divorce, we made numerous visits to check on Gail and the kids, which by then totaled three. Most often when we stopped by Gail wasn't there, only a baby-sitter. The conditions in the house were disgraceful; trash was scattered throughout it, the kids' bedroom window was broken, and there was a clear lack of hygiene. One time, the sitter was sweeping up trash in the living room. There was so much, she could've used a rake. Later on, after Gail moved out, the house was condemned.

Franny couldn't stand to see the terrible situation our niece and nephews were in. We knew something had to be done and we were the only ones who could or would take action. This was certainly evidenced later by my mother's comment, "Why didn't you just wait for the state to take them?" It was Franny's idea for us to take in all three children to live with us. I thought she had great courage to come to this decision, especially because she'd have to shoulder the responsibility. We just knew it was the right thing to do.

Fortunately, I contacted the lawyer who kept Gorman out of jail years earlier. He lived in Foxboro, was aware of Gorman's domestic situation, and seemed very well informed about the kids. Luckily, he agreed to help us pro bono and off to court we went.

In December 1966, within a few days of our court appearance, we received a call from the lawyer informing us the court order came through. I vividly remember that Franny and I had just dressed up to attend a company Christmas party at the King Philip Ballroom in Wrentham, and we immediately changed our plans. That night, wearing our party attire with the court order in hand, a cop went with us to pick up the kids. Franny and I were both taken aback when the cop commented, "This is the best thing that could happen for those kids." It seemed everyone who had any knowledge of the conditions in their home realized the gravity of the situation. I imagine it may even have been part of the town gossip.

At that time, we had four children of our own. With the addition of John, age five, Maureen, age three, and Greg, age two, Franny would now say, "I have seven under seven."

The first couple of weeks were just a blur. I remember Franny and I frantically trying to pull Christmas together for everyone. After the holidays, the workload on Franny was incredible and I was very worried she'd work herself into an early grave. After another month, I became more concerned and discussed with Franny that it was too much. My argument to Franny was, "You're working yourself to death. The result of you continuing will be that I'll be left alone with all these kids. Whom will that help?" It was truly a crushing thought for me.

With heaviness in our hearts, we decided we were only able to keep one child. It certainly was one of the most grueling decisions we ever made, but having seven under seven was an extreme financial and mental burden on our family. It was decided we would keep Greg, Franny's godchild, who was just two years old and needed the most care. John and Maureen were placed into foster care. The heaviness of this decision especially weighed on Franny's heart for the remainder of her days.

Greg fit right in and was treated like any of the others. Joe and Greg were only nine months apart in age. Somehow Joe took Greg under his wing, a level of responsibility no one expects from a two-year-old. I think this greatly eased Greg's transition into our family. I vividly remember, in their early years, Franny dressed the boys alike just like twins.

John was originally sent to an orphanage in Worcester run by nuns. Maureen was placed in foster care with an older couple in Hull. Franny and I occasionally visited John at the orphanage and Maureen in her foster home, and we tried our best to keep them in our lives. Life was certainly not easy for them. John spent too many years in the orphanage before finally being adopted around age 12 by a nice family that lived in Wellesley. Maureen endured many foster care placements and difficult situations. During the summers, we made arrangements for both of them to visit our kids on the Cape, although they didn't visit on the same days.

While I recognize Franny and I did the best we could, it pains me to this day that John and Maureen weren't given the stable home life they deserved. Despite this fact, they both persevered through it all and I admire them greatly.

CHAPTER 12

Our Growing Family

I N September 1968, once again I sat in the waiting room anticipating the arrival of another addition to our family. I remember each time while I waited for the big news, my mind was focused on Franny, hoping all would turn out well and there wouldn't be any complications. Happily, Frances Josephine Smith, our sixth child, was born healthy. We named her after Franny's mother.

With kids ranging from infancy to nine years old, Franny was a very busy woman. As crazy as it was, she held it together. One of the tools she used was assigning the kids chores to do. From very young ages, everyone had a job to contribute to the success of our household. As the kids got older, the amount of responsibility increased. Thanks to Franny, our growing family was a happy and organized one.

During my generation, most child births took place in the hospital, with the fathers in the waiting room. That certainly had been the case for me with all our children. Little did I know that was about to change.

Towards the end of Franny's sixth pregnancy and arrival of our seventh child, she started insisting I be present at the birth. Her doctor resisted, but Franny threatened to change doctors and even hospitals, if necessary. As usual, she prevailed.

There was a little hesitation on my part because it wasn't a common practice, but since it was important to Franny, I agreed. I had no idea what to expect and wasn't given any instructions. She was so excited about the prospect, and giving birth in general, that I showed excitement, but to be honest I was a bit nervous. In fact, in order to make sure my presence wouldn't have any negative effect, I vowed to leave the delivery room if there was any problem. I was determined to make sure all focus was on Franny. On August 18, 1970, I became the first father to be present at a birth at Sturdy Memorial Hospital. Shortly thereafter, it became common practice.

Being in the room when Richie, our last child who was named after Franny's brother, arrived was profound. The experience and emotional impact can't be described. I never felt so delighted in my life! To this day, I have deep regret that I wasn't present for all the others.

Franny was the driver and guiding light regarding having kids, due to her Catholic religion. She was fixated on the idea that when we wanted to stop having kids, we'd simply stop being intimate. I didn't agree. We went for counseling with a Catholic priest to work through the issues. He was very supportive and led us to a solution that allowed us to avoid increasing our family in a way that wouldn't go against the church. Fortunately, all things worked out well. Our happy family of nine was complete and lots of adventures were yet to come.

CHAPTER 13

Car Accident

I SPENT NINE YEARS, FROM 1967 TO 1976, PURSUING MY BACH-elor's degree. While I was the one attending classes three nights a week, Franny said "the whole family went to college." I considered majoring in both engineering and business administration. Night classes in engineering were only offered in Boston at Northeastern University. That would've been over an hour commute, and I wasn't able to leave work early enough to arrive on time. In addition, the extra commuting hours would've been very difficult to maintain. Since I knew I could already do engineering, but I was challenged by office politics and was told (by Franny) I was too blunt, I decided to pursue a degree in business administration. It was clear to me my engineering bosses were poor administrators and I wanted to do better. I found a program at the University of Rhode Island (URI) in Providence, which resulted in a reasonable commute. On the night of my classes, I'd head home first for a quick dinner and then dash off to school. With Franny's support, always having my meal ready and waiting on those nights, it worked out quite well.

The route I always took from Attleboro to Providence went through Pawtucket. Along the way I passed through a busy shopping area that had sidewalks and numerous shops on both sides. The route was well lit and heavily traveled.

In 1974, on a dark and rainy dark night as I passed through this area, a woman suddenly stepped off the curb in front of my car. Although the visibility was good, there was no time to react, and I hit her. She fell to the pavement, and I stopped. She ended up about 10 feet in front of my car. Lying on the pavement she looked completely normal, with no obvious injuries, blood, or signs of trauma. My car showed no signs that there had been an accident, absolutely no damage, not even the paint was affected.

Someone called the police who arrived within minutes. I stood fixated and stunned outside my car watching the commotion and emergency attention paid to the woman. At some point on the scene, the police informed me the woman had died. I got into the police car and was taken to the police station while my car was towed away. I was questioned and taken to the Attleboro border where I was picked up by the Attleboro Police and taken home. I was stunned and upset, and certainly in no shape to drive! Shortly after that, I was called by the Pawtucket Police to return to the station. Franny accompanied me to meet the detective. The three of us sat in the lobby while I answered more questions. I wasn't detained or charged with anything.

There was no further contact from anyone about the accident. I never knew or wanted to know the lady's name. To be the cause of ending someone's life is an experience one can't describe. The guilty feeling never really goes away.

This is one of those things in my life that was difficult to get over. I never wanted any reminders of the incident, so I called a junkyard who came and picked up the car. I would never drive it again.

Franny was a great comfort and support during this time. In addition, a Protestant pastor and his family lived directly across the street from us. We had a number of conversations, and he shared many words of encouragement and support, which were also very, very helpful.

Because of my situation and responsibilities, I put it behind me and moved ahead. This may sound cold, but I couldn't allow this to have a destructive impact and affect me or my family. Whenever in my past I experienced a painful situation, I'd discard the memory and go on to what was next; thus, time and energy was never wasted. This turned out to be a good survival strategy for me.

CHAPTER 14

Camp Mullin and Family Fun

WHEN FRANNY WAS A CHILD, MR. M BUILT A PLACE in East Dennis on Cape Cod for the family to get away in the summer. It was a beautiful location in Crowes Pasture overlooking Cole's Pond. Many years later after the Mullin children were grown, Franny's parents attempted to live there for one winter, but since there was no electricity and it wasn't winter-ized, it didn't go well. The only source of heat was a pot-belly stove hooked up to the fireplace. Also, when a North wind blew it was completely unprotected, which kept the house quite cold. For some period of time, Mr. and Mrs. M became house-sitters on the Cape during the winter and spent the summers in "Camp Mullin." Even-tually, they bought a lot of land on South Street about three-quar-ter mile from the camp next to Franny's youngest sister and built a year-round ranch home. By that time, all but one of Franny's siblings lived on the Cape, so the camp stood empty.

Once our oldest kids were a little more independent, Franny took the opportunity to spend summers with the kids at Camp Mullin. I stayed in Attleboro and worked during the week, then joined the gang on the weekends.

Franny and the brood were blessed with spending many summers there until our youngest graduated from college. It was a beautiful place, a small Cape house on 15 acres. It was located on a freshwater pond with good swimming and a short walk to the beach. Despite the lack of electricity, there was running water by way of a gas-powered pump and a refrigerator run via a propane tank.

All the kids have fond memories of summers there. Franny's hands were full during the week, but she managed all things well. I was very eager to go to the Cape on the weekends. I remember those Friday nights when I drove down the dirt road to the camp and saw the kids sitting on "Waiting Rock" excited to see me return.

It was a bit lonely at home, but there were lots of home repairs and improvements for me to accomplish during the week after work. One major home improvement I completed one summer was converting our single bay garage into a bedroom for the boys. It included building up the floor of the garage, replacing the garage door with a glass slider, insulating the walls, installing electrical wiring, heating, and carpeting, as well as a bookshelf along two walls, and, of course, painting. Thank goodness I had the ability to take on such a project without them home. At the same time, I had a contractor build a separate free-standing two-car garage next to and slightly behind the house. I was a busy guy!

Projects back at the camp kept me busy as well. Since our family was the primary of the camp, I assumed responsibility for its maintenance. I replaced porch boards, the pump and gas engine for the water system, and did other minor repairs and replacements.

Although I've expressed I don't ever recall being angry with Franny Girl, I do recall two occasions when she was angry with me, both of which centered around work being done at the camp. The first occurred sometime after spending summer at the camp became a regular practice. At one point, the camp needed to be painted, so I bought the paint and went to work. The amateur that I was, I somehow managed to get paint on some of the screens. Since it only affected the appearance and not the function of the screens, I figured it wasn't worth my time going back and spending more time on it. Yes, some of the screens didn't look as nice as others due to the presence of white paint, but it wasn't that bad. I had lots of other work to do, realized the error of my ways, and knew how to prevent it from happening as I continued. Franny never said anything to me about it. During the week, I returned to Attleboro to work as usual. The following weekend when I returned, I learned from one of Franny's twin sisters that the twins spent an afternoon fixing my mess and that Franny was steamed! Franny and I never discussed it.

The second occasion concerned an old car we kept at the camp for Franny. In those days, exhaust systems were plain steel and needed to be replaced much more often than now. The fact the tailpipe on the old green Rambler station wagon needed replacement was obvious from the loud engine noise emanating from it. Mr. M, my great father-in-law, wanted to help, as he often did, and spent two or three days addressing the issue. While I wasn't there at the time, I can only imagine the sight of him crawling underneath the car expending lots of effort to make the repair using orange juice cans and coat hanger wire. Franny was quite happy to report this successful repair to me when I arrived at the camp. Now, I should mention the road to the camp was a very rough dirt road, about three-quarter mile long. With me driving on that bumpy road, Mr. M's repair didn't last one trip in and out. I sure got an earful about that, in a controlled burn kind of way that Franny used to express her displeasure! Clearly, she was angry and upset because I'd swiftly undone her father's hard work.

When we were on the Cape, much to Franny's chagrin, the kids and I played a game I called "Daily Drowning." Franny took exception to me calling it that, but I called it "Daily Drowning" anyway. There was a large lake called Scargo Lake nearby. I'd gather our gang, and usually four cousins and sometimes a couple of friends from Attleboro, pile everyone into the station wagon, and go off to the lake. It was only three or four miles from the house on Route 6A. The game was simple: I tried to get them into deep water to drown them, and they tried to get me into shallow water to drown me. All our kids and cousins were good swimmers. Of course, I always lost. I never thought we were being observed by others until one time a cheer went up from the shore from bystanders when I lost. It was great fun!

An activity we did often was visiting the Cape Cod National Seashore. We'd leave early in the morning and be gone all day, stopping at different points anywhere from Eastham to Provincetown. In fact, it got to the point that when we went to the National Seashore programs, the park rangers recognized our family. We'd go to lectures and on walks and spend time at various beaches. Marconi was one of our favorites.

I remember fondly that at the end of the day, we'd stop at a picnic area and put together a meal on the little charcoal hibachi grill I took along. Most often it was something simple like hot dogs and beans, but it always seemed more delicious than anything we would've cooked at home. Franny always insisted her dog have a "Bird and Son finish," referencing the parent company of Bird Machine. At the time Bird and Son was the largest asphalt roofing company in the U.S., perhaps in the world. The kids and I joke to this day about Franny requesting her hot dogs that way.

Franny was a woman of many expressions. In addition to her calling me "Honeyman," both as a term of endearment and irritation, she used to find unique ways to get her points across. She referred to the people I associated with at Bird Machine as "Bird Brains." At times when I did something she thought wasn't so smart, she'd say, "Use your Bird brain" in exasperation. Even the way she'd tell me to change my approach to get the kids to behave or comply with a request was unique: "Honeyman, try to encourage [insert child name] to [insert desired outcome]." I could go on and on. To this day, the kids still use many of them jokingly.

Bike riding was another activity when the kids were older, both on the Cape and in Attleboro. On the Cape we'd ride down Route 6A to Brewster, about five miles away. In those days traffic was light. I'd never do it today.

Another family summer event was going to the drive-in movies down Route 134 in East Dennis. I'm sure we were quite a sight with all nine of us packed into the car. At one point, the drive-in started charging per person instead of by the carload as they always had. I remember one time trying to beat the system by putting several kids in the trunk to save money. Once we parked and bodies were piling out, a worker caught us and we wound up making good and paying for everyone. I don't think we ever went back after that.

Franny absolutely hated leaving the camp at the end of the summer to return home to Attleboro. She'd wait until the last possible minute on the evening of Labor Day, the night before school began. Even though the kids were anxious to get back to see their friends and the neighborhood, Franny was always very sad to the point of tears at times. Regardless of the timing, she always had everything in place to start the new school year. All back-to-school shopping was completed while on the Cape. She was a master organizer.

Since our return trip started so late, there wasn't time to prepare a meal. Our practice was to stop at a Burger King with a gallon of milk. One year we found a restaurant along Route 118 in Taunton, off a side road in the woods. I think it was called Tuk-Away Farm. An older couple ran the restaurant and all the patrons seemed to be in the same age bracket. The first time we went there, Francie, our youngest daughter, was an infant. As we walked in, it was apparent everyone thought pandemonium would ensue with the arrival of our brood. Fortunately, everyone behaved and had great table manners. When I went to pay the bill, the proprietor wouldn't accept payment for the kids. He said, "You folks are welcome anytime. It was a pleasure having you!" Over the years we stopped there a few more times with the same results.

Once back in Attleboro, there were lots of activities. One game I remember playing with them when they were very small revolved around me being a monster. I grabbed and tickled them and then pretended to eat them. The trick was that if anyone grabbed my big toe, I became helpless. This was a fun game, and of course, I always lost. The kids showed me when they got too old for this game by putting me down the stairs, headfirst. That was a surprise!

I remember Joe taking particular interest in bike riding. In fact, when he was a young teenager, we went to Rhode Island to ride with the Narragansett Bay Wheelmen, a biking club. They had many different routes over varying distances. I remember Joe participating in one that was 20 miles long; no one else in the family joined in on that one!

Another favorite family activity was showing home movies and slideshows now and then. Topics included various timeframes. The kids particularly enjoyed watching old footage of me and Franny water skiing before we were married, and there were lots of slides of times at the camp, sailing, holidays, my work trips, etc. The kids just loved it!

Christmastime was by far the most exciting time of year for the kids, particularly when they were young. Despite our limited funds Franny and I managed to splurge to make it special for the gang. At times we actually borrowed money to cover our expenses, which would take a month or two to pay off after the holidays. The thrill of watching the kids on Christmas was magical and truly worth it!

Franny and I felt so blessed over the years to raise our kids. Our family was a busy and happy one.

Photo Gallery

1949—Frances Mullin

1950s—Mr. & Mrs. M

1957—Vaughn Smith (top), inscription to Franny (below)

1958—Vaughn, Franny, and Gorman, Camp Mullin

1959—Mr. & Mrs. Clement V. Smith III

February 14, 1959—Franny, Vaughn, and the wedding party

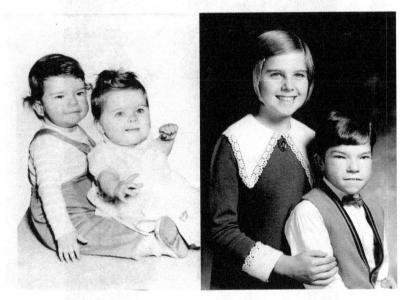

1961 (left) and 1971 (right)—Clemmy and Mary, our oldest children

1963—Mary, Becky, and Clemmy

1967—Greg, John, and Joe

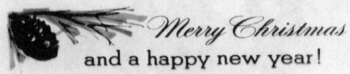

1969 Christmas Card
Back (L-R): Mary, Becky, Clemmy
Front (L-R): Joe, Fran, Greg

1969—Franny and Vaughn, Camp Mullin

1969—Becky, Fran, Franny, and Mary

1971—Mom Cushing, Vaughn, and kids

1973—Richie, Becky, Greg, Joe, Mary, Fran, and Clemmy

1974—Franny, Vaughn, Becky, Greg, Fran, Joe, and Mary

1974—Mullin siblings

Franny, Richie, Patricia, Joe, Priscilla, Billy, and Trudy

1976—Mary, Joe, Fran, Greg, Clemmy. Becky, and Richie

1978—Franny and Vaughn, Camp Mullin

PART THREE

MY WORK LIFE

1960s—Vaughn, Bird Machine

CHAPTER 15

My Two Lives

LIKE MOST MEN IN MY GENERATION, I LIVED TWO LIVES: MY home life and my work life. Perhaps my home life was more important but occupied the least time. My actual time at work was eight hours every day plus travel time and the frequent occasions I was on trips. As I look back, those two lives were completely separate. My work provided the economic means to support our family, which was the only connection between the two lives. Thanks to the Creator, I was gifted with a natural talent that made doing my job fun!

Since I relied on Franny to manage the kids and the home, I was able to focus on my work. Thanks to the Creator, Franny was a brilliant manager. She performed magic with my small paycheck and was wise when difficult decisions needed to be made. There were seldom issues between us, and when this occurred, we came to a consensus. I was always Franny's reliable back-up.

Throughout my career there were two rules I always followed, which I believe led me to success:

1. Always act in the best interests of the company.
2. Be honest, fair, and helpful to all folks with whom you work.

CHAPTER 16

Bird Machine

IT SEEMED TO ME MY CAREER ACTUALLY STARTED AT BIRD
Machine Company. Up to that point, my work life was training
for the work I did there.

Earlier jobs made me an excellent draftsman and taught me how
parts were made and the functions of all machine tools. The five years
I worked at Standard Fittings honed these skills to a fine edge. My
boss encouraged me to manage my projects from concept to production. This evoked my interest in parts of the process beyond design
and engineering. A book I read on value analysis added to my skill
set. In my entire career, I never saw anyone else use value analysis.

At Bird, I followed the same practice developed at Standard Fittings. After a short time, my bosses at Bird saw the value of this and
stayed out of my way. It was a happy and fulfilling situation for me,
in spite of the fact the compensation didn't match my contribution.
Analyzing my design and production efficiencies saved Bird, and
later Fiberprep, so much more than they paid me, it was almost as if I
actually paid *them* to work there. Oh well, at least I had job security.

The majority of my working years were spent at Bird Machine
where I worked for 26 years, from 1963 to 1989. When I started,

they employed about 1,500 people, of which 100 or so were in the engineering department. The machine company was a division of a much larger operation that employed six or seven thousand. The office was located in South Walpole, only five miles from our house in Foxboro. Bird made industrial centrifuges, filters, and accessory equipment for the paper industry. Overall, I enjoyed my time there. I was given many opportunities and the work was lots of fun!

Bird Machine made various types of machines for different applications and markets. It was divided into two divisions: paper and filtration. Filtration was by far the largest. It consisted of two products: centrifuges and filters. Centrifuges were the most active product line. There was a planetary gear unit that was a primary component on all centrifuges. There is hardly any manufactured product that doesn't have one of its components go through a centrifuge at some point during its creation.

I was hired as a designer and started on planetary gear units, a critical part of the centrifuges. I wasn't there a week when I learned Bird had a licensing agreement with a German company to build a stock preparation paper machine. The drawings were in German and metric format. The outside company being considered for this work happened to employ the sales manager who got me started in the business, my old neighbor, Jim. In my spare time I looked at the situation. I realized it was more of a logistical issue involving resources than one of engineering. I found that by internal re-arrangement this work could be done internally. I presented my findings to the powers that be, and they were accepted. Why didn't the bosses see this? This was the kind of thing I did at my job in Framingham as well: another gift from the Creator! It's interesting that I was recently hired and immediately saved the company a substantial amount of money. It seems funny now, but it didn't seem to be appreciated then.

Despite little formal training, I could solve all engineering problems that came my way. I did this by reading and developing a good engineering library. The math I lacked, I taught myself. I became an expert in gear design and developed new gear boxes, with more capacity, using existing parts we had to stock to service obsolete gear boxes that were still in operation from decades earlier.

I also made changes to existing centrifuges and filters that always reduced costs, sometimes by a lot. My past tool design experience gave me insight into manufacturing operations that were more efficient and cost-effective.

Some of my design changes were rather radical. I never gave a thought that utilizing these changes involved risk and might not work. They always worked and reduced costs! It never occurred to me that I could fail.

After a very short time, my bosses never questioned anything I did. I was given a free hand to manage my projects. Interestingly, at raise time any semblance of confidence in me didn't translate into significant additional compensation. I didn't think I was treated fairly, but at least the work was fun. In addition, I helped some folks advance their careers, which was very satisfying.

CHAPTER 17

My Working Conditions at Bird

M Y FIRST DESIGN JOB WAS A NEW VACUUM FILTER valve for a mining application. It can be best described as being like a merry-go-round, about 40 feet in diameter. The valve was in the center of the filter and all working components in the machine were stainless steel. I was responsible for the design of the valve, which consisted of two large stainless-steel castings. The patterns to make them were quoted at $25,000—too expensive! I proposed to make it a welded construction of plates, tubes, and formed components without the need for patterns. This reduced the weight by 70%. Also, many machining operations could be eliminated. I projected cost savings at 80%. My direct boss and Division Manager, Ron Sigmund, as well as Chief Engineer, Ed Garner, got involved to review my radical idea. After a brief review to ensure he had some input, Ed added two expensive operations. I felt they were unnecessary since their function could easily be solved using two simple jigs instead. Even though the operations were added, the overall savings of my design was still very significant at 70%.

After that I was happy to have the opportunity to work with the supervisor of the filter group. Ron was a great guy, a very capable engineer, who happened to be a Scottish immigrant. After the machine was built and delivered, I was asked to assist him with its assembly. It was shipped in pieces and put together on location in Canada. I flew on a small plane out of Norwood and had a great experience getting the job done. I guess I did a good job, because after that, my involvement in troubleshooting began. Bird had a dozen service engineers who serviced the equipment. If there were issues with centrifuges that the engineers couldn't handle, I became the point man, or trouble-shooter. This might entail technical as well as customer service issues. It became one aspect of my job I enjoyed the most. This took me all over the U.S., Canada, and even Europe.

An incident comes to mind. There was a problem, and the customer was irate. I wasn't briefed about this and was sent in cold. When I got there, the service engineer filled me in.

In the conference room was a large table with six or eight angry customers seated. I made a presentation defining the history of how things developed and what needed to be done to fix the problem. I asked if there were any questions. There were none. As we left, the service engineer said, "Clem, we're going to get fired." I answered, "Well, I wasn't going to lie. My integrity is not for sale." The plant manager caught up with us, tapped me on my shoulder, and said, "Mr. Smith, I want to thank you for your honesty." When I got back to Bird, not a word was spoken about it. The problem was resolved.

Another time, there was a problem with a machine in Utah. While I was there, some welding needed to be done. I noticed the welder wasn't using a welding shield. The light from welding is so bright it can cause eye damage, and a spark can cause instant blindness. The shield is dark plastic and provides complete protection. I immediately stopped the welder and had a conversation with him. Assuming he was a family man, I asked if he was married, had children, and wanted to be able to continue to support his family. He answered "yes" to all the questions, which I knew would reinforce the need to use the shield. Once I explained its important safety features and strongly urged him to use it, he continued to do so while I was there. I hope it became a permanent procedure. I should also mention his welding was first-rate.

At some point I was promoted to Project Engineer and received a small increase in pay. I was the only person with that title and did all the new design and redesign work. To support my design work, I wrote instruction manuals for the operation and maintenance of the newer, more complex centrifuges, like pressure centrifuges, which needed more specific and detailed instructions. No one told me to do this, but the need was obvious to me. I also rewrote and updated all the existing centrifuge manuals that covered the older models. I dictated the content information and sent it to our stenograph pool to be typed. To my knowledge my manuals were never edited, nor did I receive any critical feedback. At some point Ed hired a guy to rewrite a manual I'd written. Apparently, he thought someone with specialized training in that discipline would do a better job. This guy spent a year on it. In the end, he was fired, and his work discarded, while my version remained active. Funny, I never took a writing course, and I don't recall reading a book on the subject, though I might have, but my knowledge base was much stronger. Clearly as the designer, I had the best perspective to be successful.

I remember taking a trip that deserves mention. The project involved the design of a pressure centrifuge. The customer was located in Belgium. Over the course of the project, I noticed the customer specified the material for all the seals, which normally would've been done by Bird. Realizing it was the wrong material for the application, I notified the sales department, but they chose not to inform the customer. As a result, two machines were shipped in the defective state. Sometime after that, on a Friday morning, I got a frantic call from Ed asking me to go to Belgium to supervise the seal replacements. He said, "You're the only one who can do this." At the time I was attending college at URI and had a final exam on the following Monday. To miss the exam meant I'd have to repeat the course. Ed talked me into taking the trip and I took the last night flight out of Boston on Friday, arriving in Belgium on Saturday morning. I worked all day Saturday and Sunday. I don't recall much of what I did while there, but I left late on Sunday and arrived back in Boston late the same evening. On Monday, I spent time at the office then took my exam that night. I don't recall the exact grade, and I'm sure it wasn't up to my usual performance, but I passed.

One of the salesmen, who was in New York City, liked to have me along on sales calls. This was usually a monthly trip. Bird's machinery was custom made and some customers wanted special features. Oftentimes my ability to analyze the customer's needs, and identify efficient ways to accomplish them, served everyone's interests. Using my skills to make a positive contribution in this way provided me with lots of satisfaction and I was happy to help other salesmen in the same way.

At that time Bird had a number of service centers to provide repairs and service. Another aspect of my job included making numerous trips to these facilities where I wrote procedures for critical repairs.

I remember during this time, there was a recession and Bird didn't have any new orders. Then we were given the opportunity to get a large order from China. In order to do so, Bird had to host six Chinese engineers so they could observe the manufacturing process over the six-month period it took to complete the order. Bird agreed to take the order and gave the Chinese engineers free reign and access to the technical information and processes. Needless to say, after the order was completed, the engineers left with lots of information and Bird never got another order from China. I suspect scenarios like this played out repeatedly thousands of times during that time, contributing to the demise of manufacturing in the U.S.

After a few years, the engineering supervisor for the centrifuge group left and I was offered the job. Ed said, "We don't think you can do the job, but we're willing to let you try." I thought his comment was a case of "give him enough rope…" expecting I would "hang myself," but they knew I was very helpful to the previous person who had the job, so it was probably worth giving me a chance. At least they didn't get in my way. Looking back, I think the reason Ed didn't like me was professional jealousy. He resented the fact I acted without consulting him, always with a positive outcome.

After six months, the hours to complete a job by my crew of 20 (10 designers and 10 detailers) decreased by 10%, which was equivalent to adding another team of two men.

In engineering, there was a policy of not correcting errors on engineering drawings once the drawing was released. This was carried to the point that if anyone made a correction, it was a black mark at raise time. There was a formal procedure for changes, and the person making the changes, as well as their superior, had to sign. Rather than the guys being blamed for the corrections, I changed the policy so my signature was the only one required. This resulted in savings of about $25,000 a month since manufacturing no longer had to spend time reworking parts due to drawing errors. By the time my bosses noticed, they no longer cared because they realized the substantial savings. I didn't learn about the true monetary benefit until about eight years later. Not surprisingly, there wasn't praise or even an "Atta Boy" at any point in time.

My management style was different. When there was a problem, I'd have a meeting with my designers. I'd present the problem and ask for ideas for a solution. Everyone was given an opportunity to provide input. Although I had my own ideas, sometimes one of theirs was a better one. Even if someone duplicated my idea, that person got the credit. After a course of action was decided, I gave work assignments and there was never a problem getting the work done. I removed the partitions between the guys and created an open floor plan. My desk was centered in the middle of my work group so I could be accessible to my team. Morale was good and I think my team enjoyed working with me.

My direct boss treated me with disdain and I wondered why. On several occasions he indicated those who worked for him were merely "warm bodies." That seemed to be where I fit, which led me to avoid him as much as possible. After a few years of this, I considered other employment opportunities, but with no degree my options were limited. It would also mean moving, and the family was happy where they were. In addition, looking back at my experiences now, I'm glad I didn't make any job changes because I can't imagine I would've had the opportunity anywhere else to do the variety of things I did at Bird.

CHAPTER 18

The Bird Quoting System

A MONG THE DUTIES OF BIRD'S ACCOUNTING DEPART-
ment was the generation of quotes for all incoming orders.
For standard items, it was very straightforward, but for
custom orders the process seemed overly complicated.

To me it seemed the process of creating a custom quote was
structured to spread the blame across three departments: engineering, manufacturing engineering, and accounting just in case things
went wrong. Engineering marked up the drawings in red, which
went to manufacturing engineering to estimate the number of hours
required to manufacture the item. Finally, accounting calculated the
cost and mark-up to prepare the quote. Sometimes this process took
an entire month to get a quote to the sales department for presentation to the customer. This was a common occurrence and seemed
not only unreasonable, but certainly preventable to me.

To make the process more efficient and accurate, I proposed
using historical cost data to develop cost curves. We had lots of data
going back in time for the most common materials for all sizes of
machines. Using the historical cost for a specific-sized machine in
an exotic material, like titanium, I applied my cost curves to estimate

the cost of the same machine in any size. This also worked for component accessories. Using this method I completed a quote very quickly, easily within a day if I had nothing else to do, for some of the most complicated machines.

I presented this to the powers, but it was rejected. I never understood why, except for the fact the accounting department would then become solely responsible for the quoting process and therefore solely to blame. Perhaps that was the reason it was rejected.

Regardless, I continued to use my method to test Bird's quoting system by comparing the actual post-production costs to the quotes and found my estimates to be more accurate.

CHAPTER 19

Just Call Me Sam

WHILE I WAS WORKING AT BIRD, UPPER MANAGEMENT decided to have a service engineer meeting, similar to the annual sales meeting. There were around a dozen service engineers, so this seemed worthwhile. Because of the incident I'm about to describe, this was the only such meeting ever held.

During my time at Bird, I was often called to join service engineers to solve machinery and customer problems. So, I got to know all the service engineers, some very well, and we all liked and respected each other.

I was assigned the task of presenting information to the service engineers over a five-day period. My goals were to get feedback on new designs currently in process and provide updates on changes to existing designs.

The meeting was held in a hotel in Charleston, West Virginia. The service engineer I knew best was Clyde Riddle who was a redneck from South Carolina. He was a capable, nice guy, but a bit of a racist. The hotel arrangements were two to a room; Clyde and I shared one. Directly across the hall was the service engineer department manager who roomed with a new service engineer. Charlie, the manager, was a very proper, straight-laced guy and a deacon in his church. While the group went to the bar, Charlie stayed in his room watching TV. He wasn't a good fit.

The second night there, everyone but Charlie gathered at the bar. I nursed a beer while the rest got "feeling good." Clyde suggested we play a joke on Charlie by getting a naked hooker to walk in on him. The planning got pretty loud and we called over a black hooker who worked at the hotel and was seated at the other end of the bar. She joined the group, and a deal was struck. When asked her name, she said, "Just call me Sam."

She came to Clyde's and my room and got undressed. The new service engineer had a key, so we had access to Charlie's room. Sam had a funny idea to use a sheet and act as Charlie's "guardian angel."

Since we couldn't see in, we relied on her account of the interaction. As she described it, she walked in, opened up the sheet, and proclaimed she was his guardian angel. Sam said Charlie's eyes got as big as saucers, and he pulled up the sheets to cover all but his face. After a minute or so, he composed himself, jumped out of bed, and pushed her out the door. He pointed to our room and yelled, "You're in the wrong room. You're supposed to be across the hall!"

We all had a great laugh. Charlie didn't take it well, which only made it funnier. He threatened to fire everyone. Most of the group wasn't concerned, but a couple were very anxious. I told them not to worry about it.

Every evening after that, Sam joined the group in our room. The beer and the booze flowed liberally, and she told us stories of her life. She was from Pittsburgh and was a hotel employee with regular benefits, healthcare, retirement plan, etc. She claimed the hotel was owned by the Mafia and she was shuttled between Charleston and Pittsburgh depending on business needs.

When we returned to Bird, Charlie threatened to fire anyone who mentioned the incident. The new service engineer quit. Clyde thought the story was too good not to pass around. No one was fired and we all had a great laugh.

CHAPTER 20

More Bird Stories

DESPITE THE MANY GOOD THINGS I DID AT BIRD, THERE was never one word of encouragement; it was just the opposite.

Through my interest in value analysis, I came to understand that a man working with his own tools costs less than a machine and operator. The value of the machine could be hundreds of thousands of dollars. At Bird these costs were a fixed average rate for all operations: a distortion of the costs.

There was also a huge quality problem. Bird manufacturing insisted on half-welding the bowl of the machine. This meant there was an unjoined part of the cylinder, which was half the total thickness on the highest stressed part of the machine. Strength calculations made on the bowl, due to the rotation of the machine, showed the stress was double!

One of the old timers at Bird told me that in the distant past, a failure of the bowl occurred completely destroying a customer's building. Since the centrifuge was usually run unattended, luckily no one was hurt. To give you a perspective, the Bird centrifuges weighed anywhere from 500 to 50,000 pounds. The larger units were much more in demand. I tried to get the half-welding process corrected for years, but after being promised in numerous meetings it would be done, it never was. Finally, a welding engineer was hired, and I got it done.

Regardless of my position, I always considered that I worked for the sales department. If it doesn't sell, they don't need me. So, I always tried to get a sense of what I could do to improve our sales position in the market.

One day out of the blue, I was "promoted" to Product Manager and transferred to the sales department. I never found out what I was supposed to do, except hold down a desk and collect a paycheck. There was no need for this position, or even a job description, and I only remember doing one thing during that time. Bird had a licensing agreement with a German company that had a technical breakthrough. I was sent to Germany to create a detailed report on the technology transfer. I wrote a 24-page report that was used by the Bird engineering department to duplicate the technology. Shortly thereafter, I was transferred to another position to manage contract administration and service—boring!

CHAPTER 21

My One Patent

THROUGHOUT MY TIME AT BIRD, I CONTRIBUTED MANY designs that could've been patented, but the process wasn't pursued. Around 1985, 22 years into my employment, that changed. During my time in the sales department, I assisted on sales calls to address technical questions with potential customers. There was a very serious wear problem on machines used in large mining applications. A "wear committee," of which I was a member, was established to study and solve the problem. At first, the engineering department was not represented. A little later, a newly hired designer was assigned. I think the new hire was selected because he wouldn't have any connection or loyalty to me.

The first problem we tackled was the screen section. This was solved by using many pieces of formed tungsten carbide. I don't recall where the idea came from, but I solved the problem of how to make it after many detailed discussions with the vendor who was to supply it. Somehow, the new hire got the credit. I was annoyed, but didn't want to take the time, effort, and energy to fight that battle. I was never any good at office politics.

The biggest wear problem centered around a major component

on the machine that required complete replacement every three months. This component was the support shafting and main bearing on one end of the machine. It was protected by wear plates that under normal conditions protected the part for the life of the machine. Disassembly of the machine was required to replace this major component. With downtime and parts, the maintenance cost was probably one-third to one-half the total cost of a new machine.

One of my friends on the committee held a doctorate in mechanical engineering from MIT. We worked together on a number of projects with great results. At MIT, he found a master's thesis that evaluated impingement angles on wear. He gave it to me to see what I could do with it. Using the principles in the thesis, I redesigned the major component using replaceable parts of wear-resistant material in areas subjected to wear. As a result, these replacement parts needed to be replaced only once every three years and the machine didn't have to be disassembled. In addition, the down time was reduced to a few hours and cost less than $2,000. In contrast, the previous design required a $10,000 investment every three months, resulting in a cost of $120,000 over the same three-year period—an enormous savings!

I did all the drawings myself, and only the sales department was involved. Having read a few patent descriptions over the years, I wrote the patent application, following the same format and style I'd seen. I also created the necessary illustrations. Because my preparation was so complete, my meeting with Bird's patent attorney was cancelled since it was deemed unnecessary. The final patent description differed little from my write-up. I take pride in this accomplishment.

Around 1987 or 1988, Bird was losing money. No one in top management seemed to know why. A committee of three was formed, including me. The other two guys wanted nothing to do with it. After one meeting, I realized the committee wouldn't be productive. I knew what needed to be done to address the situation, so I volunteered to transition to Chief Estimator to be solely responsible for gathering data and assembling quotes, thereby eliminating the need for the committee, which was subsequently dissolved. I established a new quoting system using my cost curves and historical data. Working with the sales department, I updated the price book and established the mark-up. The lead time, the time from order to payment, was six months. Interestingly enough, the time it took for Bird to get "back in the black" was exactly six months, the time that elapsed after processing the first order based on my quoting system. No one acknowledged my contribution; once again, no raise, no "Atta Boy."

By that point I'd honestly had it with Bird. The raises I got throughout my time there were pitiful. Fortunately, it was enough to support a family, though in a frugal state. After I left Bird, I learned other supervisors made substantially more.

CHAPTER 22

Work After Bird

I N 1989, AN OPPORTUNITY PRESENTED ITSELF. A SALES MAN-
ager from Bird, Ed Healey, left and started a company in Taunton,
which was an easy commute. The new company, Fiberprep, made
machines for recycled paper stock preparation. Ed's knowledge base
was unique because, while at Bird, he served as the sales manager of
the paper division for many years then, for a shorter time, as the sales
manager of the centrifuge division. Since the paper and centrifuge
divisions were run separately, it was rare for people from the two
divisions to interact. It was during Ed's years in the centrifuge division that we got to know each other. Ed knew what I could do and
hired me as Chief Engineer.

After a meeting assessing sales projections, I put together a budget
to cover personnel needs. I needed three people in addition to the
guy Ed, unbeknownst to me, originally hired to be the chief engineer. Nelson also came from Bird but seemed to do very little work
at Fiberprep. I wrote job descriptions for my department, hired the
folks, and went to work.

I was hired at the same pay as my last position at Bird. Shortly
thereafter, I discovered Nelson's salary was substantially more than

mine. I brought this to Ed's attention and got a 75% raise. Looking back on it, I think Ed low-balled me just to make sure I really wanted to be there and would be loyal.

The machinery was to be built under license from two companies, one in France, the other in Japan. The first job was to design a piece of machinery that was a large tank of stainless steel. Using stress analysis, I calculated we could save $7,000 in materials alone by making some minor changes to the original design we received from France. When I presented this at a meeting, Nelson said, "You will change nothing, not one screw or piece of material." Ed responded, "Did you hear what he said? I'll take the $7,000!" Other changes resulted in over 25% cost reduction. In one case of re-design, cost savings were 85%. There were no complaints, returns, or warranty problems. This was true for my entire career.

Since all drawings had to be converted from metric to inches, this was a great opportunity for re-design. In one case I improved function by re-designing a shaft assembly so it could be replaced as a single unit, which needed to be replaced every six months. We offered these as replacement parts. If customers purchased them, it would save about eight hours of down time. I also wrote the instruction manuals with necessary drawings.

While I was quite competent at my job, I was incredibly blind to office politics. Looking back now, I think a couple of incidents that happened early on at Fiberprep illustrate that. The first one involved the first installation of my new tank design. I was told by our sales manager, Bob, who was from Bird's paper division, that our first customer complained the de-inking tank material was "too flimsy." I was tasked to meet with him in Canada. When I got there, the tank was full and operating and I was told the guy I was to meet with was unavailable and not interested in meeting with me. So, I returned home and submitted my report for the wasted trip.

Shortly thereafter, we were installing a centrifuge we bought complete from our French licensor. It ran at the same speed as a

Bird centrifuge of the same size. The customer wanted to mount the machine on the second or third floor of their building. Specifications for mounting a large centrifuge were on the ground on a large concrete block. For installations inside buildings, Bird solved building mounting issues by placing the machine on springs. The reason for this was due to the fact that all centrifuges are, at times, unbalanced due to the loads they process. A slightly unbalanced centrifuge has a natural frequency near that of the building. This can actually bring down the building. Installing it on springs changes the transmitted frequency, solving this problem. This installation was the first time Fiberprep used this type of spring mounting application. I was told by Bob that the customer was incensed at the idea! Once again, I was tasked to go for a site visit to the mill in the Midwest to meet with the angry customer. When I got there, everything was running smoothly and, once again, the customer was unavailable and not interested in meeting with me. So, I returned home and submitted my report.

Ed was copied on all my reports. I didn't think about it then, but thinking about it now, I believe office politics played a role. This is what I think happened: Nelson and Bob both came from Bird's paper division. They knew very little about me, aside from the fact that I didn't have an engineering degree, not even a two-year. Nelson was side-lined out of the chief engineer position so Ed could hire me to fill the role. I believe Nelson and Bob set me up so Nelson could reclaim my position. I'm sure they expected I'd fail, especially with my radical ideas.

Shortly after the second wasted trip, Nelson left. I think Ed realized what was happening, showed Nelson the door, and told Bob to knock it off. After that, things went smoothly, and everything worked well. How naive was I?

My team worked well together. Our engineering clerk was a woman, which was very unusual. I always thought a woman could do the job better than a man because I think women are better at assessing and paying attention to details. Vivian Taylor proved my point. Her kids were older and in school. I don't remember her background, but this was her first job after staying home with her children. Vivian did a fantastic job! At raise time, I always gave her a big boost. She was so good that near the end of Fiberprep in Taunton, the company president hired her as his administrative assistant.

John Blake was my number two. I passed new designs on to him, and he finalized the design and got it ready for manufacturing. He was a very reliable, hard worker who was with me until the end of Fiberprep. We became friends and are still in contact today.

The other man, whose name I've forgotten, left us after four years or so. I replaced him with a recent Worcester Polytechnic Institute graduate who was with us for the duration. He was a very nice young man. I learned later that he became a schoolteacher.

Since we had no manufacturing facilities, and I was responsible for quality, I traveled periodically to meet with our manufacturing vendors. I wrote lots of procedures for quality control, which eventually evolved into a quality assurance manual. I enjoyed delving into the manufacturing side of things. I learned a lot from one Canadian manufacturer who offered suggestions for minor changes. We interacted frequently, had many fruitful discussions, and enjoyed each other's company. Together we solved many problems and saved both companies money. I also traveled to meet with our licensors in France and Japan.

After a few years at Fiberprep, I noticed our customers were using a computer software drafting program called AutoCAD. I sent my guys to school and they taught me. At first, we created basic installation drawings the customer used to design the facility to house the paper pulp preparation systems. Then we created detailed manufacturing drawings for the component manufacturing process.

Around 1997, Thermo Electron Corporation, the conglomerate who financed the creation of Fiberprep, bought a larger company, Black Clawson, in the same business. It was decided Fiberprep would merge with it. Black Clawson was located in Cleveland, Ohio. I sure didn't want to move to Cleveland, and I didn't feel ready to retire, so we parted ways. Of all the places I worked, Fiberprep was the most fun overall! I truly enjoyed the autonomy I was given, was treated very fairly, and was compensated well.

After Fiberprep, I did a little consulting work and looked around for another job. During that time, Bob hired me as a consultant. I guess after working together for eight years, he figured I knew what I was doing. After leaving Fiberprep, he started a parts replacement business for Fiberprep parts. I consulted with him for about seven years and gained a lot of respect for Bob during that time. Prior to leaving Fiberprep, he had an accident that left him paralyzed from the waist down. Despite the difficulties, Bob found the strength and fortitude to keep going and start his company. I don't think I could've persevered the way he did.

One day, Franny was looking through the PennySaver and saw a small ad for a gear designer at a company called Velvet Drive in New Bedford. They made transmissions for boats and forklift trucks. Since it would be an easy commute, I applied for the job and was hired as a project engineer. Once onboard, it looked like the company was on its last legs. Fortunately, it lasted five years.

There was a problem with Velvet Drive's boat transmission that had been going on for nine years! There were lots of rejected parts on the production line and potential warranty problems. After I was there a year or so, they wanted to increase the horsepower capacity of this transmission. Since gear changes use hydraulic clutches, a higher-pressure spring was needed. I was asked to design the spring. To avoid the necessity of study and tedious calculations, one could simply ask the spring supplier to duplicate the existing spring but increase the pressure. The problem with this approach was that the natural frequency of the current spring would've been duplicated, which wouldn't have solved the problem. Through calculations I discovered there were three choices of natural frequency. I could duplicate the existing, go higher, or go lower. Drawing from my knowledge of isolation systems for centrifuges, lower was always better, so that was my choice. This solved the problem, and they were impressed! I admit it was a bit of a lucky guess that worked out for all. I guess when I'm not good, I'm lucky.

In 2002, after five years there, Velvet Drive closed. I did a little consulting but was basically retired.

1990's—Fiberprep ad in trade magazine

PART FOUR

MORE YEARS, MORE STORIES

2009—Me and Franny, 50th wedding anniversary celebration

CHAPTER 23

Boat Stories

IN 1976, WE BOUGHT AN UNASSEMBLED WHITE 20-FOOT Luger. I spent about three intense months assembling it in the garage. It came with instructions but, after reading a dozen books on fiberglass to learn about construction, I made some modifications. I remember being challenged by the centerboard. If you're not familiar with sailboats, the centerboard is a retractable keel that pivots out of a slot in the hull that allows the centerboard to be raised in shallow waters. It also makes it much easier to trailer the boat and was a feature I used and appreciated often.

I had to cut a slot in the hull where the centerboard would go through. The original design included using a gazillion screws to hold the centerboard trunk—a sleeve inside the boat where the centerboard resides—to the hull. Instead, I took the trunk pieces that went together and sanded off all the gelcoat to expose the fiberglass. Then I put a fiberglass mat between them and dropped the centerboard trunk onto it so it was like one cohesive piece. This redesign was a lot stronger and made the centerboard trunk much more rugged. A winch was used for cranking the centerboard up and down. The original design called for the winch to be located in the center on top of the trunk, which interfered with the companionway. I decided to move the winch back underneath the companionway, so it was completely out of the way. I then created a pulley system to accommodate the distance from the winch to the centerboard. It was a great improvement.

After the Luger was operational, we went cruising for a week every summer. Franny's sister, Priscilla, and her husband, Pete, had a boat of similar size, so we cruised together. On a typical day, we'd start with a quick bowl of cereal for breakfast, then we'd get underway to our destination. Among our ports-of-call were Block Island, Martha's Vineyard, Cuttyhunk, and Nantucket, as well as a few places on the mainland. Sometimes one or two of the kids came along. It was a tight fit, but it worked. When we reached our destination, we explored the area, and in the evening, we'd find a nice restaurant for dinner.

A few years after we got the Luger, I subscribed to a boating magazine. My subscription included the ability to contact others with similar interests by mail. This was long before faxing or email. I began corresponding with a man in Pennsylvania who had the same kind of boat we had, and we arranged for him and his wife to join us on a cruise with their boat. Pete and Priscilla joined in their catboat as well, and all three boats spent a delightful week sailing to Martha's Vineyard, Cuttyhunk, and similar locations. I don't remember a lot about the Pennsylvanians, but Franny called them "Mork and Mindy" after a popular TV show at that time. He was a former Air Force fighter pilot, a retired major. His wife's name was, in fact, Mindy and they didn't have any children. We traded letters for a time after our adventures. Last I heard, they purchased a 45-foot sailboat and were on the way to the Panama Canal, intending to sail around the world.

We owned and enjoyed the Luger for many years. It was a great boat, handled really well, and we never had any real mechanical problems. It could sleep four people, although it was tight, and you had to be very friendly to do it. When at Camp Mullin, we often used it as a daysailer, trailering it over to Sesuit Harbor. The family would get in and we'd go out sailing. I remember one breezy day when almost everyone was on board. We were sailing upright while other boats were healing to one side due to the strength of the wind; we had the advantage of using the kids as great ballast to keep us upright.

Once Franny became weaker and couldn't walk very far, we needed a boat big enough to carry her wheelchair. The Luger was just too small. In 1985, my brother-in-law rented space and a building next to a boat storage and repair business that had a 26-foot 1971 Balboa for sale. It was big enough to fit a wheelchair, slept four, and had a separate head section. Even though it was just six feet longer, it was twice as big in terms of weight and volume, yet still trailerable. All loaded up it weighed about 2,600 pounds which was quite a contrast to the 1,500 pounds of the Luger.

In good condition, the Balboa would probably have cost about $10,000, but I ended up paying only $3,000 since it had been damaged in a hurricane. It was set to be my new project. There were holes in the sides of the hull, the deck was messed up, the bottom of the rudder was broken off, and more. It was definitely something I would describe with my well-known comment, "So many problems." The rudder damage presented a unique challenge because I had no idea how long it was supposed to be. At the time, I was writing to a guy in Alaska about the repair work needed and I mentioned not knowing what to do about the busted rudder. He sent me a pattern to follow to lengthen the rudder, which worked quite well.

I spent a full year working tirelessly to restore the Balboa. My youngest son, Richie, helped as well. There was lots of fiberglass work and reconstruction, but with my experience I felt like I knew what I was doing. I also made lots of interior changes and improvements, including installing fabric on the inside of the hull to replace the original finish.

I was absolutely consumed with getting it ready for the next boating season. Every night I'd come home after work, grab dinner, then head out to the yard to work on it. Franny said, "All you do is work on that damn boat!" It was very rare for her to say a word like "damn," so I knew she was quite irritated with me.

The exterior needed an entirely new paint job. I knew a guy at Bird who worked in the manufacturing engineering group and worked part-time painting cars. He told me he could spray the boat for me. I picked out a bright yellow color, similar to the original, and bought the paint for $300, which was very expensive in those days. I remember feeling like it was ready to be painted and having the guy come down only to tell me I hadn't sanded it down smoothly enough. In the end, he did a great paint job and the boat looked like new on the inside and out.

We had many great trips on the Balboa. It was great fun for all. When on our sailing trips and arriving at our destination, we usually anchored out. You'd think this caused a problem for Franny, but fortunately she only weighed 120 pounds, so I was able to help her into our dinghy and back onto our boat.

I called every boat we owned, even the daysailers, *The Dreamer*, although I never physically put the name on any of the boats. However, the bright yellow color of the Balboa encouraged lots of comments and jokes from the kids. At some point my son-in- law, Wally, Mary's husband, started calling it *The Clemon* (obviously a combination of Clem, my nickname, and lemon) and it stuck.

We still had the Balboa when we moved to Wareham in 1994, but by then Priscilla and Pete weren't going on trips and Franny wasn't up to it. I sold it to a guy who couldn't believe the quality of work I'd done to restore it. I still wanted to do some sailing, so I bought a smaller boat, a 19-foot Cruisers Incorporated motorsailer. With a big enough motor, you can water ski behind a motorsailer, but we never used it in that capacity. It needed a bit of work, which I, as usual, enjoyed doing. I had it for a few years and fixed it up so it sailed well.

In 2005, my son, Joe, saw a 22-foot Macgregor listed online. That was the last boat I owned. After solo sailing it for a few years, I experienced some medical issues and it sat in the yard more than I used it and started to deteriorate. By that time that size of boat was a bit out-of-fashion. I tried to give it to Mass Maritime for their auction, but they weren't interested, having just recently taken one to the landfill. I sold it for little to no money to a guy who was so happy to get it that I didn't feel too bad. By that time my son, Joe, and his family had a 32-foot Hunter that I'd go out on occasionally. Because the boat had a walk out transom, we were even able to get Franny on the boat for a few sails. Being able to spend time out on the water with Franny again felt great and reminded me that the boat's name, *La Dolce Vita*, or *The Sweet Life*, certainly reflected mine.

CHAPTER 24

Franny's Disease

IN THE LATE 1970S, WHEN FRANNY WAS ABOUT 45, SHE started showing symptoms of the same condition as her father. Mr. M's main outward sign was a funny gait, but he never used a cane. He had a drop foot on both sides and lifted his leg up higher than normal to take the next step. The degree of impairment remained at a constant level and didn't seem to worsen during the time I knew him. Franny's two older brothers, Billy and Richie, started with the same symptoms when they were also about 45. To my knowledge, there wasn't an official diagnosis for her brothers or father. Although affected, Mr. M was completely independent, did his own shopping, etc. until his death at the age of 85. This wasn't so for Franny and her affected siblings.

As soon as Franny showed signs, she went to Rhode Island Hospital for evaluation. After a week there, filled with many tests, she received the diagnosis of myasthenia gravis, a chronic autoimmune, neuromuscular disease. Although the classic symptoms are weakness of the facial muscles, she didn't show signs of that. Her symptoms were limited to her extremities. Regardless, Franny was treated for myasthenia gravis with prednisone, to which she responded well. After a year or two and a conversation revealing her father's symptoms, which had previously not been disclosed, her doctor questioned his diagnosis and sent her to the foremost expert on neuromuscular diseases at Massachusetts General Hospital in Boston.

The Boston doctor diagnosed her condition as Charcot-Marie-Tooth disease, also known as CMT, a hereditary neurological disease affecting the peripheral nerve cells and their ability to send information from the limbs back to the spinal cord and the brain in order to activate muscles. The degeneration of the nerves results in muscle weakness and loss of muscle in the arms, legs, hands, or feet. Franny's symptoms were classic CMT: gradual weakening of the muscles in the arms and legs. Since prednisone had shown some benefits, the Boston doctor decided to jack up her dosage more. Although it helped a little, it also caused her face to swell and brought with it many possible long-term side effects, including deterioration of her bones. After a couple years with no significant improvement, she got off the drug. I think it was the right choice, especially because prednisone was never shown to be, and isn't prescribed today as a treatment for CMT.

While we accepted the CMT diagnosis, Franny and I both always questioned it. Even so, we labeled her condition as such, and the kids even referred to it as "The Sharky Tooth."

The prolonged prednisone treatments were known to weaken the bones. In addition, her muscular condition deteriorated, affecting her balance and setting her up for a fall.

Franny always hung clothes outside on the clothesline. We had a dryer, but it was seldom used. In December 1988, just weeks after the birth of our first grandchild, Joel, Franny was hanging up clothes when she fell and broke her hip. Greg found her when he came home, called the ambulance, and she was off to the hospital. The hip replacement surgery over Christmas was a success and Franny seemed to recover quickly. I remember being at home with the kids for the first time without her on Christmas. She was always in charge of getting the gifts and had done so that year as well. The problem I had was knowing exactly which gift was for which kid. Joe and Greg, being as close in age as they were, seemed to always receive similar gifts. Since I had no idea what to do, I put the same tag on two gifts for them which read, "Boys, you figure it out." It became a joke for years to come.

Then in 1992, while Franny was on the Cape at the summer place, she fell and broke the other hip. Our youngest son, Richie, who was working his way through college, found her in the yard and took her to the hospital. Fortunately, that hip replacement also went well. Franny used a cane after that.

In December 2009, when genetic tests were available, she was tested for CMT. The test covered 14 types and all results were negative. I've heard there are now at least 21 types, so Franny's results aren't 100% definitive.

Other data that supports my theory centers around Franny and her six siblings. Since her father had it, we know it's genetic. Although Mr. M, Franny, and her brothers all developed the disease in their mid-forties, her younger sister, Trudy, didn't develop it until about age 60. Looking further down the family tree, you find that from the four siblings affected there are 20 offspring, *none* of whom show any signs of the disease.

Here's my conclusion (for what it's worth): Franny's disease, like cancer, required a trigger to activate it. The trigger was present in her generation, but not the current one. I believe her disease hasn't yet been identified or given a name, and since few are affected, and it's difficult to track, it's unlikely to be studied.

What might the trigger be? In Franny's generation, houses were heated by coal with a coal bin in the cellar. In addition to coal dust, there was exposure to the fumes. Later, homes were heated by oil or gas, which burns a lot cleaner. I think the timing of the coal exposure is a possible source or trigger. In fact, Mr. M upgraded their home from coal to oil heating at some point, and the six-year difference between Franny and Trudy may have reduced her exposure, allowing for a delayed onset. So, that's one possibility, but I think we'll never know.

CHAPTER 25

On to Wareham

AROUND 1988, WE REALIZED THE RAISED RANCH wouldn't work for us long-term. Our multi-level house and the frequency with which Franny contended with too many stairs presented obstacles that were increasing to unrealistic levels. So, we discussed and searched for a suitable home elsewhere. Franny wanted to live on the Cape where there was limited opportunity for employment for me. Living costs and real estate prices were higher there, so it just wasn't feasible. We looked on the mainland side and found Wareham to be the best location, particularly with its access to major highways. Over three years, we spent many weekends looking at houses. Finally, we found a residential lot Franny liked. It was on a dirt road and backed up to a salt marsh with open water leading to Buzzards Bay. The road was fairly high, but the lot elevation dropped quickly, which troubled me. At first, I had misgivings about it, but inspiration from Franny and my imagination convinced me, and we bought the 1¼ acres lot on Squaws Path in 1991.

Designing the house was a fun project for me. Inspired by Franny's desire for a bow roof Cape, a design came together. The slope and elevation of the lot, and its need to meet certain regulations relative to mean high tide, was one of the biggest challenges. I adjusted the elevation so the cellar was a walkout and brought in a lot of fill to make the front yard slope down to the road.

We decided to purchase a modular home versus a newly constructed one, because it allowed for a larger footprint at about the same cost in line with our budget. In addition, the construction timeline was a bit shorter. The modular house was constructed in two basic pieces to be assembled onsite. Then the garage and bow roofs, on both the main house and garage, were constructed. It took a little over a year for all construction to be completed.

Our new home, where I reside to this day, is modest at less than 2,000 square feet. There's a larger than average two-car garage with room for expansion of living space above. If one wanted to finish the cellar, the house could be expanded to a little over 3,000 square feet. I call it "the house love built."

Our house is a ¾ Cape. Inside, the ceilings are a little higher than normal, which makes the inside look bigger and the outside smaller. The proportions are just right, and I've received many compliments on the design.

Inside, the first floor has two bedrooms and two three-quarter baths. To anticipate Franny's future needs, the master bathroom includes extra grab bars and towel bars. The back half of the house is an open floor plan, including the kitchen, dining area, and living room. I purposely designed the doorways to the master bedroom and bathroom with wider openings to accommodate a wheelchair, should Franny ever need one, and made sure the handles on all doors in the house were lever handles to ensure any loss in Franny's grip wouldn't be a problem. There's a laundry closet with a stacked washer-dryer, and a deck off the back with a patio underneath. Franny always had to have a clothesline, so I installed a 75-foot reel-type clothesline off the deck. To this day the kids joke about how crisp the sheets and towels were when they came off the line. The beautiful view of the salt marsh and open water in the back has always been one of our favorite features. It was especially nice when my boat rested on a mooring out back.

In 1994, Franny and I, and a couple of our grown kids who were in college, moved in. The upstairs, with two bedrooms, a sitting room, and a full bath, was basically unfinished but was well used by our college commuters. They helped with much of the inside painting and finish work. With one quarter of the second floor open, we could admire the bow roof from inside, which was one of our favorite features.

Like most homes, while it was built on a budget, it exceeded the original estimates. Regardless, it served us well. The house was perfect for Franny's evolving situation and the upstairs provided accommodations for family visitors.

Life with my Franny Girl in our new home was delightful. I went sailing in the summer and skiing in the winter and always came back to her. Life could never be better than this!

CHAPTER 26

More on Dad

SOMETIME AFTER WE MOVED TO WAREHAM, I RECON-
nected with a neighbor who had lived in a condo in Pensacola,
Florida when Dad and Ilse lived there. He related an interesting story that shed light on an incident my father experienced during
his time at the Bureau of Public Roads. Once while Dad was working in Boston, he heard of a shady deal by a very high-level politician,
whose name would be a big surprise. This prominent individual was
buying land where the on-and-off ramps would be on the Route 128
expansion to later be sold to the state at a huge profit. Apparently,
Dad mentioned it to a fellow colleague, which was a mistake. The
next day, on the way to his office, Dad was met in the elevator by
two thugs. They said, "If you mention the deal again, we will kill you,
your family, and anyone else you may have told." Dad was stunned!
When he got to his office, he got a call from someone higher up in
the state bureaucracy. I'm not sure where this person fit on the orga-
nizational chart, but he was later prominent on the Big Dig Project.
He told Dad he needed to resign from the Bureau of Public Roads,
which he did. I was in high school at that point. The story Dad told
at the time was that he didn't get along with his boss and decided to

resign. He then worked for a major contractor in Boston for about five years. After that, Dad was rehired by the bureau, with full benefits, as if he never left. He was immediately transferred to Laos for a period of 1-1/2 years. I don't know exactly what he did during that time, but he and Mom returned before the start of the Vietnam War. His next assignment was back in Washington, D.C. where he remained until his retirement. By then he had been promoted to Inspector General of the Bureau of Public Roads, the highest level he could achieve without requiring a presidential appointment. This makes me wonder whether it was his actual talent or the act of keeping the incident that led to his departure quiet that contributed to his steep rise to the top.

In 1964, while my parents were living in Springfield, Virginia, just outside Washington, D.C., Franny and I took the kids to visit them. Franny was pregnant with Joe at the time, experiencing morning sickness, nausea, and generally not feeling well. Clemmy, Mary, and Becky were toddlers, and Grandma was the babysitter while Franny and I took trips to D.C., about twenty minutes away, to see the sights. Overall, it was a pleasant and fun trip.

My parents visited us several times while we lived in Foxboro and Attleboro. During their visits, my mother stayed around and visited the kids, but Dad left after breakfast to do other things, then returned for dinner. I remember there were very limited interactions between him and the kids, but the visits went quite well and it was nice to see them.

My mother passed away in 1972, in her sixties, due to heart issues. I always felt my mother was a bit of a "crushed soul." I think years of being treated as a servant and abused by my father took its toll. With our large family, it would've been very difficult for Franny to accompany me, so I went alone to the funeral. I actually don't remember a church service, but I do recall a relatively small indoor gathering, and that there weren't any heartfelt tributes shared.

Two years later, Dad married a nice German lady named Ilse.

She was a former model, the widow of one of Dad's golfing bud-dies, and a golfer herself. She didn't have any children. Dad asked Franny and me not to attend the wedding, so we didn't, but I do know that Gorman was invited and did attend. Ilse told me months later that my brother said to her, "You'll never replace my mother." I responded, "It's been a long time since I needed a mother, but I sure could use another good friend." And so, we remained friends for the rest of her life.

I was happy for them. Dad and Ilse had a more compatible rela-tionship than he and Mom did. Although Dad still had a booze problem, Ilse didn't partake. She didn't tolerate any nonsense from Dad and seemed to have his respect. When Dad and Ilse retired, they moved to Pensacola. Franny and I visited them there.

Dad had Alzheimer's in the last five or six years of his life. Ilse managed this, and Franny and I were very grateful, since otherwise that task would've come to us. After Dad passed in 1995, Ilse and her niece, Julia, traveled from Florida to visit us in Wareham. We were so grateful to Julia for taking care of Ilse in her last years. Ilse died in 2009.

I recently discovered more information about my father's family. For years I've been in contact with my first cousin, Bill Moore, who lives in Atlanta, Georgia. Recently he discovered, via AncestryDNA, we have a first cousin named Pam, who is the daughter of one of Dad's younger mystery sisters. I called Pam, who lives in Oklahoma, to connect and we spoke for an hour. The story is that both of my mystery aunts were placed in an orphanage, presumably around the time of my grandmother's breakdown. Pam's mother, Nellie Brook-smith, was a nurse in World War II. It seems that Aunt Nellie never discussed her sister, who Pam never met. More recently, I learned from Bill that my other aunt was placed in an institutional facility at some point which was where she died. It makes me wonder if per-haps she was similar to Clemmy.

CHAPTER 27

Preparing the Kids for Adulthood

FROM THE BEGINNING, I WAS THE DISCIPLINARIAN IN THE family. Franny reported actions and behaviors and served as the guide as far as my actions were concerned. In those days, discipline was physical, the same way it was when I was a child. I used my hand when the kids were small and a belt when they were older. I remember hearing the phrase "spare the rod, spoil the child," which means if a parent refuses to discipline an unruly child, that child will grow accustomed to getting his own way and will become a spoiled brat. I think it came from the Bible, but I'm not sure. It was a popular sentiment at the time, and I never questioned it. Until recently I never considered my actions made my kids fear me or caused a wedge. It may have been my greatest fault as a parent. Fortunately, I have a pretty good relationship with most of the kids at this point. I'm glad my kids saw my faults and didn't emulate them with their own children.

Shortly after starting night school at URI in 1967, I began feeling the strain of my increased schedule. After working all day, taking classes three nights a week, doing homework, and being a family man, I was tired and feeling rundown. Following a conversation with a coworker who had experienced a similar rut and found that running midday was the key to regaining a healthy energy level, I started running a couple miles at lunchtime each workday and sometimes on weekends. At home I had two loops: one was seven miles, and the other was eleven miles. My solo running time was almost like a meditation, a good chance to ruminate over work issues and other thoughts. Overall, it gave me lots of energy and kept me in shape and in good health. At some point, it became a part of my routine and improved my energy level to such an extent that it never occurred to me to stop running at any age. It became a life habit that I continued into my 80's until health issues intervened and I was reduced to walking. I also think it certainly helped to maintain my weight over the years. In fact, I'm still close to the same weight I carried during my senior year in high school.

Although I didn't set out to do it, I believe my commitment to physical fitness contributed to the fact that almost all the kids became runners or hikers or skiers, and generally physically active adults in some way. Two of the kids, Greg and Francie, even ran the Boston Marathon. So, I think I had a positive influence on them in this area.

Franny and I were more intentional with the kids in other areas. When the kids were older, in preparation for driving there were things both boys and girls were required to learn: master the ability to change the car's motor oil every 2,000 to 3,000 miles, including the filter, as well as perform an engine tune-up every 15,000 miles. This consisted of changing spark plugs and changing and setting the points in the distributor. Another requirement was changing a tire, which was more challenging back then because the spare tire was full size. We were proud they all learned to do this well. It was just part of our commitment to making sure our kids would be strong and independent.

Having responsibilities around the house was another area of focus for us. Franny was in charge of doling out the indoor domestic chores. The kids were assigned various tasks like washing and drying dishes, changing sheets, dusting, vacuuming, cleaning bathrooms, and taking out the trash. Outside, I included the boys in most property maintenance tasks: mowing the lawn, raking leaves, shoveling snow, painting the house, carpentry projects, etc. Overall, I think it had a positive impact on them, although when Mary was in her teens, she told me she learned all the swear words from me when I was working on projects when things didn't go so smoothly.

Franny hung a calendar on the inside of a kitchen cabinet where the kids wrote down who had what chores during the week. For washing and drying the dishes, they were paired up for the week and chore assignments switched on Saturday night. Franny and I were even included in the washing and drying rotation. I remember on a few occasions the kids tricked us into doing dishes for an extra week. It would be a Saturday night and one of the kids would turn to me and say, "Looks like it's your turn tonight." Even though it seemed like I'd recently been on washing dishes duty, I'd shrug, say "Okay" and start washing. It usually didn't last more than one meal, or a day or two, until the kids fessed up and cracked up. They really got us good a few times.

Our goal was to instill the kids with a strong work ethic, and I think we succeeded. Although I remember having my doubts at times when something happened around the house, and no one owned up to it. I'd ask, "Who did this?" Inevitably, the responses were a continuous string of, "I didn't do it." My line then became, "Nobody ever does anything around here." There was one time in the early 1980s when our oldest, Mary, was dating her then boyfriend, now husband, Wally. He visited our home in Attleboro with the entire family present. All the kids were downstairs watching TV. When I went down, I noticed the window in the back of the room was broken. Though I knew it was a rhetorical question, I asked, "Who did that?" Immediately Wally confessed, saying, "Well I did," to which the kids, almost in unison, immediately snapped at him with words to the effect of, "You never admit that!" In the end, the kids became a hardworking and pretty confident bunch, open to learning new things and always trying to do their best.

Except for Clemmy, for obvious reasons, our kids attended and graduated from college with bachelor's degrees. Three also earned master's degrees. I'm so proud of all of them!

Since Franny's and my resources were limited, we were unable to be of much financial help. Although we provided room and board, they all had to work part-time to get through college. Among the jobs were roles as waiters, waitresses, prep cooks, landscapers, a bus tour guide, and a marine electronics technician. Most of the kids commuted to school to save money. Only Mary, whose college was too far for a commute, graduated with significant college debt that took years to pay off. She never told us about it. In fact, I only learned about it recently and was a bit shocked and very impressed that she never wanted to burden us with that knowledge.

All the kids make a good living, and we were proud as parents to cheer them on! But what our kids did isn't possible today. Instead, most college graduates have huge loans. The part-time jobs our kids worked to get through college have now become careers. It's a sad reflection on where we've come as a country. I'm certainly grateful to the Creator for the timing for my kids.

Franny and I often told the story of how we met and discussed the process of selecting each other as life partners. I always hoped the kids would realize the importance of being sure to know your potential partner very well. In my generation the divorce rate was extremely low but now has grown to over 50%. I'm happy to say our kids are happily married to the one with whom they started. I think and hope Franny and I set a good example!

CHAPTER 28

Traveling

In 1984, for our 25th anniversary, the kids sent us on a trip to Bermuda. We were both thankful for their generosity and really enjoyed the trip. It was extra exciting for Franny since it was her first airplane ride. We stayed at a great hotel where everything was included. Our accommodations were very comfortable, which we enjoyed, and the food was exceptional. In fact, it was so good that I gained eight pounds, which took me several months to lose after the trip.

This was in the early days of the onset of Franny's condition, and I noticed her endurance was limited. We rode the bus, but there was some walking to see the sights. I remember one time we had to slow down and have a short rest period. I think this was a surprise for both of us. There's lots to see in Bermuda and we had a wonderful week there.

Our next trip took place around 1981 or 1982 after I was sent to Moab, Utah to fix a machine. I needed a piece of a special alloy, monel, but it hadn't yet arrived for me to use to fabricate the part. Multiple shipping delays resulted in me having lots of time on my hands while I waited. Since Moab is the central location for several national parks, each day I took my rental car and toured the parks. Wow! I was impressed!

On Friday, when the alloy still hadn't arrived, I was told to return to Bird. When I got home, I told Franny, "You have to see this place!" Quickly thereafter, I put a trip together and even rented a wheelchair. Franny could walk fine, but not that far. Since I traveled a lot, I accumulated frequent flier miles and our flights were practically free. The hotel wasn't expensive, and I knew the best restaurants. We explored more extensively than when I was there. We had a delightful seven days seeing the sights. Until this trip, Franny had seen only the eastern part of the U.S.

In 1999, for our 40th anniversary, the kids sent us on a cruise. Once again, thanks to their generosity, we explored together, and I introduced Franny to the Caribbean. We traveled by plane from Boston to San Juan, Puerto Rico to board a cruise liner. We departed from there and visited many islands. The ones I remember best are St. Lucia, St. Kitts, St. Croix, and St. Thomas. I found St. Thomas to be the most interesting since I lived there for about three years in my youth. We hired a cab to take us around. Surprisingly, there seemed to have been only minor changes over the years. When I lived there in the late 1940s, I was told the population was around 5,000. At the time of our visit, I was told it was five times that. I was surprised since it seemed to me the change in population wasn't reflected in the changes we saw. There didn't seem to be any construction or expansion. On an island that was four miles wide by 13 miles long, I'd expect an increase in the population to that extent would be quite evident, but it wasn't. The small Catholic school I attended was the same, yet the high school was gone. My impression from our brief visit near the main town center was that little had changed.

Unfortunately, the tours of the other islands were by bus and not set up for the handicapped. So, aside from seeing the towns in the main ports-of-call on the other islands, we didn't explore further on any island other than St. Thomas. Still, it was an enjoyable trip.

Despite our trip to the Caribbean, Franny had no interest in traveling outside of the U.S. Her preferred mode of travel was always riding in the car with me driving. So, in the early 2000s, when she expressed an interest in seeing Niagara Falls, I put together a trip so we could drive there.

On the way, we stopped at Lake George, New York and took a boat tour. I remember the tour guide pointing out a number of homes that were said to be owned by celebrities.

We drove through Buffalo, which was formerly an industrial city. It was distressing to see the decline and abandoned buildings. It reminded me of cities like New Bedford, Massachusetts, whose thriving business economies had deteriorated.

When we got to the falls, we discovered they were best viewed from the Canadian side, so we ventured there. It was truly a beautiful sight to see. There was a boat ride to the base of the falls, but we had no interest in that. I would've loved a tour of the large hydro power plant there, but none was available. We stayed on the U.S. side and spent a few days seeing the sights and exploring the area.

On the way back, we toured a ski area in Lake Placid where the winter Olympics took place in 1980. We both enjoyed the fun trip and each other's company.

CHAPTER 29:

My Wonderful Life and Franny's Passing

FRANNY WAS A LOVELY WOMAN. AS SHE AGED, SHE BECAME more beautiful. When we married, she had long hair. I thought it looked great, even when she got out of bed in the morning. After we settled in, she had it cut shorter, and I thought it looked even better. Most unusual was her summer transformation when she became a blonde. I remember early on seeing her experiment with makeup, which she seldom used. I told her, "That's not an improvement. You can't improve on perfection." To that I got the eye roll and she rarely, if ever, used makeup other than lipstick again.

Every now and then after we were married, I'd bring her flowers, sometimes for occasions, sometimes not. At some point, she asked me not to get them anymore and I don't recall exactly why. So I started with a little jewelry. After a while, she seemed to have more of that than she needed and most of it remained in its boxes.

I then transitioned to buying her clothes. I'd go into stores, like Macy's, and if I saw something I thought would look good, I bought it. More than half the time she actually liked what I bought. It was really never for a special occasion. I just thought she had a great figure and wanted to help her show it off, even after six kids and two broken hips. This was true for most of her life. She was so beautiful but never seemed aware of it. Lucky me!

Throughout our marriage we had a very close, harmonious relationship. While we certainly did disagree and had arguments on occasion, we never had any big angry blowouts like I knew other couples did. I'd like to think we always had calm, respectful civil discussions. While tension and frustration may have flared, because of our love, we had profound respect for each other and always worked towards consensus. Once a course of action was decided we were both on board, 110%, with mutual support. Together we were responsible for the outcome, whether good or bad, and there was never a blame game.

I've heard it said, "There is no such thing as a perfect marriage." I beg to differ! I never thought our life together was hard. We had challenges, perhaps more than most couples, but together we made decisions and Franny made it work, day in and day out!

I pray and give thanks every day for my wonderful life with Franny. Our meeting was a miracle that couldn't have happened but for four incidents that lined up in time and space: (1) my car accident and loss of license, (2) the breakup with Kathy, (3) going to Moseley's instead of to dinner with Kathy's family, and (4) Franny going to Moseley's without her friend that night.

Thanks to the Creator for my wonderful life and many, many blessings!

After all the kids graduated from college, we were "empty nesters." In 2015, we both developed health problems, Franny with her disease and me with my heart. Back in 2010, I had a heart valve repair, but now a different valve needed to be replaced. In preparation for my surgery in early January 2016, I went to live with Joe and his family in Rhode Island in late December 2015. I recuperated there as well, staying for a total of about eight weeks. Franny couldn't stay at home on her own without me, so she stayed with Francie and her family. The distance was really hard on both Franny and me, so Francie worked with Franny's doctor to get Franny temporarily placed for respite care in a nursing home near me in Rhode Island for the last three weeks of my stay. Fortunately, I saw her daily. Unfortunately, her physical condition seemed to be declining. Once I was able to return home on my own, she still needed lots of care and I wasn't yet strong enough to care for her by myself. So, we moved her to a nursing home nearby our home in Wareham. Once there, Franny began to thrive with the hope that she could return home with me. Unfortunately, it didn't work out immediately as planned.

While exercising on an elliptical trainer in our basement at home, I collapsed and fell to the floor. I hit my head, causing a large gash on my crown, and got a small fracture in my upper spine. Since I was taking blood thinning medication the bleeding was excessive, so I called 911. At the local hospital I was told my fall was caused by a heart attack, and they discovered I had fluid in my right lung. I was then sent via ambulance to Tufts Medical Center in Boston where they drained a liter of blood from my lung and observed me for four days. After being treated at Tufts, I wore a hard brace that fit together to cover the front and back of my chest, like a turtle shell, and I needed to spend time in a rehab facility. Luckily, the facility Franny was in could accommodate me. Not only did Franny and I spend three weeks in the same facility, we even shared the same room! The funny thing was that for years, the kids had referred to this nursing home as Whispering Pines, the place where old folks go to spend their final days, and jokingly threatened to send us there. How ironic it was that we were now there together. During that time, we both worked very hard to get stronger. Shortly after I came home, Franny joined me.

What followed was a wonderful year and a half or a little more. She was home and I had the ability and privilege to take care of her. I never thought of it as a burden. I loved the time we had together and was very thankful to have her near. We were especially grateful to be present, in the summer of 2016, at the wedding of our eldest grandchild, Joel.

I treasure memories of this period. During that time, I never wanted to be away from her for an instant. I was actually fearful to not be there. I didn't even allow her to stay home alone; she was stuck with me. As she got weaker and couldn't walk very far, even with her walker, I'd either push her in a companion wheelchair or we'd go to places, like Walmart, that had electrical shopper carts for her to ride. I think she appreciated the feeling of independence when driving the cart. Whenever we used the companion chair, we'd joke about how it was my only opportunity to ever "push her around." Even when it became too difficult for her to make it to the store entrance, I'd drive the cart out to her in the parking lot. I think the time she spent waiting for me to return was probably the longest period of time we were apart in that year and a half.

Early in November 2017, she wasn't feeling well. She had gastro-intestinal issues and was no longer interested in eating. Eventually she was diagnosed with an ischemic bowel and an operation was out of the question. She passed away on November 12, 2017. I'll miss her the rest of my life, but I'm very thankful for our 58 years together, which gives me some comfort.

Since Franny passed, I have friends I meet for lunch once a month. One friend is the widow of a ski buddy who passed. At a recent meeting she said, "In spite of Franny's disease and health problems, I never saw her without a smile on her face." I answered, "I think and hope I had a part in that."

On a sympathy card, a niece on Franny's side wrote, "You two showed all of us what marriage is supposed to be like!" That was a really nice compliment, especially since I didn't think she knew us that well.

CHAPTER 30

A Letter to Kathy

FOR YEARS I WANTED TO CONTACT MY OLD GIRLFRIEND, Kathy, to see how her life turned out. I'm actually grateful to her for dumping me. Had she not done so, I wouldn't have met Franny. I'd never say that to her because I wouldn't want to hurt her feelings. The ending of our relationship was a painful experience, but it led to the greatest love and joy I could ever imagine. I think it was more divine guidance.

At one point I mentioned writing the letter to Franny. She encouraged me to track down Kathy, but I didn't think it was appropriate. After Franny passed, I decided to try to locate Kathy on the internet but had no luck. A couple of my kids also tried and got the same results.

I wrote this letter and would mail it if I found her.

Dear Kathy,

I don't know if you remember me. Way back in your high school days we dated. You used to call me Jimmy; I guess you didn't like Clement or Vaughn, my given names.

After three years of going together, you dumped me. You may recall my last words to you were, "You'll never find anyone who will love you as much as I do." There are times in life when it's better to be wrong.

I imagine you had expected anger from me that day. Contrary to what you might have thought, although I felt crushed, my wishes were still that you'd find a loving partner with whom to share your life. Love is strange that way, at least for me. I wish and hope you found someone who loved you as I did, perhaps even more.

Two years after our breakup your mother invited me to dinner; I didn't think it through and accepted impulsively. Only when I was getting dressed to go to dinner at your house did I consider what I was doing. I was crushed when you dumped me and I realized I could never trust you not to do it again. It would forever poison any relationship between us, so we never would've worked. I didn't call, and of that I'm guilty. I apologize and hope there was little discomfort or distress due to my absence.

For me, love was a great mystery. I wondered if I'd be able to love another as I loved you. As it happened, on the very night I missed your dinner, I met the love of my life. She was intelligent, wise, and even witty. She was also beautiful. We married and raised seven kids. They all turned out to be amazing and very successful! Also, those who married are still with the one with whom they started. I give my wife Franny all the credit for this. I helped a little. I'm so proud of all of them!

As for me, Franny always seemed to manage everything well on our income. All our kids went to Catholic school. We even were able to put aside enough for retirement. After we had the family, I went back to college and earned my four-year degree. I always enjoyed my work and was very good at it.

Unfortunately, Franny had a neuromuscular disorder. It was progressive and started around the age of 45. As her condition worsened, we made adjustments to accommodate her needs.

She passed away in 2017 at the age of 85. I miss her every day, but we had 58 wonderful, happy years together.

I hope and pray your life has been as happy as mine. I'd love to hear from you.

Best wishes,
Jimmy

CHAPTER 31

Ode to Grammy

I THINK THE BEST TRIBUTE GIVEN TO FRANNY, WHICH really describes how special and unique she was, was a poem written and read by my daughter-in-law, Egidia, at the reception following Franny's funeral. Egidia spoke with all my kids to be sure to include many of their favorite memories and expressions. While you may not understand some of the lines and inside family jokes, it certainly allows Franny's essence to shine through. I think it's a brilliant tribute to Franny and I'm very, very grateful to Egidia.

Ode to Grammy

She was born in the Roslindale house on a hill.
Being one of a motley crew of seven was truly God's will.
With Mumma and Daddy they escaped to the Cape,
Where they spent summers and holidays in the pretty landscape.
After high school on to TC she went,
Meeting Vaughn at a ballroom: an evening well spent.
58 years and 7 kids later,

We're gathered here to honor a life that couldn't be greater.
From Canton to Foxboro to Attleboro they grew,
Taking care to make sure things did not go askew.
Tasks were aplenty; lots of chores for everyone.
Honeyman had to encourage the kids to get the work done.
Gobs and smears were not allowed, don't cha know.
"Do it with a little life in ya!" not just so-so.
Always be smart. Use your mind and less brawn.
Try to know what to do. The Bird brain must be on.
The opposite of efficient and considered a crime,
Was completing a task a chocolate chip at a time.
Laundry was hung outdoors in the cold;
The sheets nicely crisp, but the towels hard to fold.
There was a schnauzer named Maxi that just had one eye,
And a Fuller Brush lady who would sometimes drop by.
If you joked about grandeur and treasures on earth,
She'd say, "Get out of McCloud's and come down to Worth's!"

Camp Mullin in summer was her favorite place to be,
With fresh salty air and the sounds of the sea.
Singing on Blueberry Hill, moments time can't diminish,
Like requesting her hot dog with a Bird & Son finish.
There were high tide swims, time on the beach strolling:
Passing flotsam and jetsam while out sailing and gunkholing.

In spite of the Sharky Tooth, she was always upbeat,
Cracking me up when she bent in half, her face near her feet.
The fact that she was affected was not cause for charity.
It was rather the opposite: an excuse for jocularity.
"What's happening?" was how she greeted us all,
Anxious to hear our news, whether big or small.
But please be polite. Try not to balk.
Speak about nice things. Stop the horrid talk.

Under her placemat her office and mailroom presided.
Filled with the free source material it provided.
Shear volumes of info you could not supplant,
Even when her dinner plate rested on a slant.
Speaking of dinner, if you made her a meal with garlic aplenty,
She would graciously state, "Oh, I don't care for any."
But when it came to treats, the finest of suppers she'd think,
Would be animal crackers and cocoa to drink.

Now, if you're going to transport your boat over land,
Grammy would tell you to make sure you have the balls on hand!
If you want your conversation with her to go south,
Ask her about using the toothpaste that stings her mouth!
I remember in the '90s about faxing we did chat,
Then she quickly responded, "You can't do that!"
More recently she'd smile with the smirk of a cat,
And sarcastically ask, "Well isn't there an app for that?"

Grammy, you're a woman of beauty, class, and grace.
There is absolutely no one that could ever take your place.
While I could go on with the homage I'm expressing,
Now it's your turn for your final blessing.
So let's raise a glass. Gong da gong gong.
She's now in your grace. God, guard and protect Mom.

CHAPTER 32

Clemmy's Story

CLEMMY'S LIFE WAS INHERENTLY FILLED WITH CHAL-
lenges, although early on he wasn't aware, nor did they
clearly present themselves. As part of his evaluation in his
younger years, his I.Q. was measured at 60. While it may have been
low, we considered him to be a relatively smart boy. He performed at
about a second-grade level but didn't progress beyond that.

I remember at one point, Clemmy became very occupied with
playing with a house built from wooden toy building blocks, two-
by-four scraps, and pieces of Masonite. He'd then take many of his
Little People figures, who he called his people, and play with them as
the family that lived in the house. This family lived as he did: when
he got up in the morning, they got up; when he went to bed at night,
they went to bed; when his dad got home from work, their dad got
home. At some point, activity by the other kids kept resulting in the
house falling down. I'd like to think it wasn't deliberate, but I don't
know. There were lots of kids in one relatively small room, so it was
bound to happen on occasion. One day, he obviously had enough.
Out of frustration, he took Elmer's glue and glued the house
together, as well as to the thick carpet and the wall. It was a couple of

days until it was discovered, by which time the large amounts of glue were totally dry. Even after removal, the glue remnants remained. When Clemmy focused on something, he became very determined. That was true for his entire life.

In his early years, Clemmy fit right in with the rest of the brood without any obvious differences. As the years passed, I think he was smart enough to see what he was missing. I imagine he became frustrated seeing his siblings grow from infants to being able to do things he'd never be able to do. Since we had a large family, this happened many times.

In his teens, Clemmy's behavior started to become a problem. He'd take things from his siblings and often break them. This behavior was targeted more at his youngest siblings, since developmentally they were closer to him, and they were most affected. His patience level declined. At some point, one of the older kids was assigned to watch him when he was outside; no one liked this duty.

We tried everything we could think of. We talked to him and had meetings with Clemmy and all the kids. We even tried counseling with the whole family. After three or four sessions the counselor said, "You have a very intellectual family. Clemmy can't see himself as part of that."

Clemmy's behavior continued to become more problematic. Finally, I saw the destruction of our family and couldn't stand to watch it. I told Franny I was going to move out if we didn't take some action. This finally got her attention.

There was a group home starting up in town and Franny was able to get Clemmy placed there. In order to do so, we needed to legally assign him to become a ward of the state. I learned later that Franny considered getting an apartment for her and Clemmy, but determined it was not financially feasible. Thinking back, I guess Clemmy was the major source of disagreement between Franny and me. Fortunately, we worked through it together.

After Clemmy was placed in the Attleboro group home, within a few years he was transferred from one group home to another, until he was sent to Taunton State Hospital, a mental health facility, and placed in the locked ward. While I remember him being at Taunton State, I only learned about him being put into a locked facility while cleaning out paperwork after Franny passed. He was put on anti-psychotic drugs and, after about six weeks, there was a miraculous change to more normal and acceptable behavior.

Once on medications, Clemmy had regular appointments with a psychiatrist every three months. The purpose of these appointments was to make sure the meds were working and to monitor his behavior to see if more was needed. Franny and I always attended every appointment through the years.

Over the course of his life, he probably lived in a dozen group homes in various towns including Attleboro, Canton, Easton, and Taunton. As a ward of the state, we didn't have any say in the changes to his living situations. On many occasions we heard stories of some of the mistreatment he received, including molestation by a fellow client and employees stealing money from him, even going so far as to obtain an ATM card and withdraw funds in the middle of the night.

Throughout those years, while we had no true control over Clemmy's life, Franny became his biggest advocate. She dedicated herself to communicating with the group homes regarding Clemmy's care, development, and safety. Regardless of her frustration level, Franny never backed down. She escalated issues up levels of command to seek action and became very adept at influencing outcomes. While she was usually successful, it was a purely exhausting experience and occupied much of her time. Clemmy certainly benefited from her efforts. I can only imagine what happened to those who didn't have a Franny Girl in their corner.

In the mid '90s, Clemmy experienced some health issues related to his heart and it was decided the time had come to have surgery to fix his ventricular septal defect. After the surgery, it was obvious he felt better physically, and his demeanor improved. He was more amenable and much less reactive and grumpy. Clemmy always had a high tolerance for pain and discomfort and didn't like going to hospitals or to see doctors. I expect he'd been suffering for a while and didn't want anybody poking at him, but clearly his condition had been deteriorating. It was clear the surgery gave him a bit of a fresh start.

While in a group home in Taunton, he made many friends and worked in a workshop called Road to Responsibility (RTR) for adults with physical or mental disabilities. He did exceptionally well at RTR. In fact, in 2002 he earned the Cory Kent Achievement Award for being the most improved client at RTR. This was a really big deal since the workshop had about 500 workers in numerous locations, and he was number one out of 500! There was a big out-door award ceremony in Marshfield that our entire family attended. We also threw him a big party and proclaimed the date of his award, July 6, to be termed "Clem Day" from then on.

When I designed the house in Wareham, I included a separate bedroom and three-quarter bath on the first floor so he could visit us on weekends. This practice went on for many years, and we all looked forward to it.

In March 2010, Clemmy, another client, and a staff member who was driving, were returning from playing basketball when a car shot out in front of them. All but Clemmy walked away unharmed. He was severely injured and taken to Morton Hospital in Taunton. After a short time, he was taken by med-flight to Brigham and Women's Hospital in Boston. If I had to guess why his injuries were so bad, it was probably because Clemmy was lying down in the back seat in his seat belt. He often did this when in the car with us. At the hospi-tal they removed a kidney and discovered he'd suffered two strokes and a heart attack. After several weeks, he was moved to a rehabil-itation facility in New Bedford where he spent six months. During that time he was fed solely via a feeding tube. After rehab, Clemmy was confined to a wheelchair and could only eat ground food and thickened liquids for the rest of his life. He was placed in a critical care group home in Taunton where he was provided with a hospital bed, custom wheelchair, and recliner. All that could be done for him was to keep him safe and comfortable.

Shortly after Clemmy's accident, my son-in-law, Wally, was watching a morning TV show and saw an interview with a young man named Quinn Bradlee who wrote the book *A Different Life: Growing Up Learning Disabled and Other Adventures*. As Wally looked and listened, he noticed similarities between Quinn and Clemmy. Wally shared the information with Mary who carefully approached Franny and me to ask for permission to reach out to the doctor who diagnosed Quinn with a very rare genetic condition, similar to Down's Syndrome, called Velo-Cardio-Facial Syndrome (VCFS). Interestingly enough, while it's termed a genetic condition, most of the time neither parent has the syndrome nor carries the defective gene. Mary wondered if having that information might help with Clemmy's treatment plan following the accident. Mary contacted Dr. Robert Shprintzen at Montefiore Hospital in New York via email, and he asked to see a picture of Clem. In response, the doctor replied he could "with 95% certainty, say that Clemmy had VCFS." While the diagnosis was good to have, it unfortunately didn't provide any value to his care. I wonder if knowing it years earlier would've benefitted Clemmy.

The period after Clem's accident was an unhappy time for him, as would have been the case for anyone. He suffered that whole time and there wasn't anything physically that anyone could do to make him comfortable. Franny and I went to see him every Saturday to watch TV or just visit. We hoped our presence would simply let him know we cared, and he could count on us.

Getting the final settlement from the insurance claim took an excruciatingly long time. Seven years passed by the time it settled in 2017. This was particularly frustrating since the lawyer we hired originally told us it was a "slam dunk" and the sizable proceeds would greatly improve Clemmy's life for his remaining years. As part of Franny's and my estate plan, a trust was established to handle any money awarded to Clemmy. The disbursement of funds, if not handled properly, could result in the loss of all his state-provided benefits. So, we hired a lawyer, the same one who set up our estate plan, to handle this aspect since he was very experienced with laws related to people with developmental disabilities. Unfortunately, the settlement lawyer did a very poor job. The limited funds Clemmy received were spent on replacement medical equipment and legal fees, and he didn't live long enough to take advantage of the entire settlement. After his death in March 2019, the remaining funds were given to the State of Massachusetts to pay Clemmy's outstanding medical expenses

After Franny passed, Francie became Clemmy's health care advocate and did a marvelous job. During one of our conversations about him, Francie told me Clemmy had been a danger to his siblings during a difficult time in his teenage years while we lived in Attleboro. She was angry because she thought I knew and didn't act to remove Clemmy sooner. She found it hard to believe Franny hadn't told me, and she said, "You two were so close, talked about everything, and made decisions jointly." I couldn't believe I didn't know. Clearly, Franny knew what my reaction would be. Had I known at the time, I would've had him committed permanently. Even after the meds took effect, I would never have trusted him. So how do I feel about this? In the end the only thing that counts are the results— Clemmy progressed and became a valued member of the family. It worked out in the best possible way for all concerned. Thanks to Franny and the Creator I didn't know.

After Franny passed, I continued to visit Clemmy every Saturday or Sunday without fail. It was a routine I thought was important for him and for me.

After Clemmy's funeral service, many people from his group homes and day programs, past and present, came up to me and expressed how much they loved Clemmy and the positive impact he had on them. It was something I didn't expect.

In some ways I feel like I wasn't a very good father to Clemmy. I guess I didn't take the time to appreciate some of his traits, particularly in his later years, and I don't feel good about it. Some of my kids have told me Clemmy had a great sense of humor. Somehow, I wasn't even aware of that, and I guess I couldn't make the connection at that time. It's unfortunate I never saw it and the other kids did.

When Clemmy was really young, I don't think I treated him any different than the others. But when his behavior changed, I think I became suspicious and demanding. I was the one who always said no. With Clemmy I was always more rigid, when I probably was more flexible with the other kids. It was easier and more routine with the other kids, which worked more easily for me, but with him it didn't. He required a different mindset that I didn't have, but looking back, I wish I had. I resisted the way Clemmy was versus the way I wanted him to be and didn't provide what was needed. I don't believe I handled things as well as I should have. The other kids had a better understanding and management of Clemmy than I did.

There was a lot of Clemmy's later life that I missed. I think I worked too hard at staying in the parent role, so I never thought of him as ever being grown up. I feel a bit guilty about not doing the job I was expected to do. I wasn't a total failure, but I came damn close. It's just one of those things that's way too late to change.

CHAPTER 33

Family Update

AFTER GORMAN'S DIVORCE, HE AND I WERE OUT OF contact for over 40 years. At some point he re-established a relationship with his daughter, Maureen, and my son, Greg. When Clemmy died, Gorman appeared with his current wife, Sydni, at the wake. I was cordial but didn't have any plans for future contact. Recently, we reconnected and now stay in contact talking on the phone, going out for meals, or having visits at my house. Johnny, the name he now goes by, seems to be doing well and has a good life. I'm happy for him.

His first wife, Gail, went through a long period when her life seemed to fall apart. We didn't see or hear from her during that time. According to her, she experienced a nervous breakdown. That certainly explains why she never visited the kids. At some point she straightened out her life and got a job with a state agency. Just before Greg graduated from high school, she called and wanted to meet with him. Over the course of many years, they began building a relationship, which continues to this day. She's now retired and has joined our family for holidays and gatherings over recent years. I'm so pleased she was able to turn things around and create a life for herself.

Recently, in a conversation with Gail, she revealed that at one point during a conversation with my father, he said to her, "The worst mistake I ever made in my life was my two sons." I'm not sure what to make of that. I think both Gorman and I felt that our parents thought we were in the way. I expect that he, being so much younger than I was, struggled a bit more with trying to make Dad happy, whereas I really didn't care and was happy we at least got our "three hots and a cot." A comment like that also reinforces the feeling I have of my father being someone I'd describe as a despicable coward. Yet, in spite of the person I thought he was, I still loved him.

John, Greg's brother, has been married a number of times, and has some children. He's worked for various municipalities in Massachusetts and owns a home on Cape Cod. I don't see John very often, but when I do, he's very pleasant to be around. He's very bitter towards his mother, and more so towards Gorman. I hope he's able to find peace with his past someday.

Maureen, Greg's sister, grew into a very warm, caring, and responsible woman. She's married with children and has relationships with both Gail and Gorman. This is a WOW! It shows a depth of character I don't think I'd have in the same position. I'm proud of her. I always look forward to seeing her and her husband, Rob.

After graduating from the University of Lowell with a bachelor's degree in chemical engineering, our oldest daughter, Mary, was hired to work in a large paper mill in Maine, and still works there today. She and her husband, Wally, a true jack-of-all-trades, had one child, Joel. Joel got a systems engineering degree from the Maine Maritime Academy and presently works for a solar power company in western Massachusetts. He's married to a lovely young woman, Brittany, and is responsible for making me a great-grandfather. Finn, their oldest, was born just nine months after Franny passed, and Hudson arrived in December 2021. Both are beautiful blessings.

Becky graduated with a bachelor's degree in earth science from Bridgewater State University. She got her master's degree in geology from the University of Maine. She's married to a fellow geology major, an adventurous guy named Andy. They have two beautiful daughters, Gwendolyn and Emma. Gwen graduated from the University of Southern Maine (USM) with a bachelor's degree in women and gender studies. Emma graduated from USM with a bachelor's degree in communications and media studies. They're quite a bright and happy bunch.

Greg joined the Navy after high school and served ten years, three years active duty and seven years active-duty reserve. When he got out, he earned a bachelor's degree in history from Bridgewater State University and went on to the University of Rhode Island, where he got his master's degree in urban planning. He has worked for various municipalities. Greg lives in Massachusetts with his lovely wife, Grace, and daughter, Olivia, who is currently enrolled at Babson College. They have lots of fun together.

After high school, Joe joined the Coast Guard and served five years active duty followed by another five years active-duty reserve. When he got out, he went to the University of Massachusetts (UMASS) and graduated with a bachelor's degree in electrical engineering techology. He married Egidia, a very creative woman. They have one very talented daughter, Michelina, who is studying theatre and directing at Fordham University. They live in Rhode Island and are the only active sailors in the family—luckily, they still let me join in from time to time.

Francie's career path was longer than the others, but certainly the most impressive to witness. She progressed from a nurse's aide to Bristol Community College to get her LPN, on to UMASS to get her RN, and recently earned a master's degree in nursing informatics from Excelsior College. She and her innovative husband, Jim, live in Massachusetts with their daughter, Genevieve, a high school student who is quite musically talented. Francie served as the health care proxy for Franny, Clemmy, and me, and we would've been lost without her.

Richie, our youngest, got his bachelor's degree in biology from UMASS. He's now a senior cancer researcher at the University of Utah. He and his hardworking wife, Chrystal, have a son, Malcolm, a very thoughtful and mature elementary school student. Richie, who was my ski buddy during his high school years, still enjoys the sport today.

All our kids worked hard and are successful. They're also just really nice people and, frankly, folks I'm proud to know. Our grandchildren have always been a particular source of joy. I'm continually astonished by their growth and accomplishment and amazed to see what evolved from the union of Franny and me.

CHAPTER 34

Spirituality and Ghost Stories

LTHOUGH I DON'T BELIEVE IN ANY FORMAL RELIGION, I do believe there is a divine Creator. Since I don't know how this all works, others may have it right; therefore, I respect other religions and those who practice them.

Franny was a very religious Catholic. I supported her and made an effort to maintain consistency for the family. I attended church when our children were young. I always thought it was important that young children learn the vital character-building lessons in their early years taught by established religions. Our kids even went to Catholic school. This was Franny's idea, to which I agreed. Once the kids were older, I figured the foundation was set, and since I didn't feel a connection to the church, I'd be better off sitting in the car and reading a book until the service was over. So, that's what I did.

Later, once the kids were grown and gone, I seldom joined Franny in church. When her disease impacted her mobility, I'd walk her in and get her seated, then go back to the car. At communion time, I'd go back in to walk her up front to the altar.

We always parked in the handicapped area. After returning to the car to wait for Franny, there were elderly ladies who seemed unsteady on their feet. I often offered my arm to walk them into the church. This was a regular practice for me. Once, Franny asked me, "What are you doing out there?" I responded, "Picking up chicks." When I explained, she chuckled.

Although Franny did, I can't accept the Christian concept that there's only one sacred text, the Bible. While there's certainly some wisdom in it, it's not something I've ever been able to buy into. I believe there's a Creator, but I don't have any insight. While I don't understand organized religion, the infinite intelligence strikes me as plausible. I believe we are gifts of the Creator. I acknowledge we have free will and can screw things up, as we often do. I know I don't have the answers and I respect others' beliefs. Whatever works for any individual works for them.

When I look at the sky and the heavens, it seems to me there has to be some guiding intelligence. I'm certainly not saying I know what's going on because I don't. But I strongly believe I have a divine guide who has steered me through my long and happy life.

Shortly after Franny passed, I started going to the Spiritualist Church in Onset whose practice comes the closest to what I believe. To those unfamiliar with this church, its basic belief system follows the Judeo/Christian morals and ethics. It has ten specific beliefs. There are two I strongly believe. First, each individual is responsible for their own happiness or unhappiness. Second, we're here to help each other. In addition, the church respects all other religions.

The weekly service consists of a sermon, healing service, and half hour of readings by mediums, most often from other locations. The entire service lasts an hour and a half, followed by a social gathering that lasts from thirty to sixty minutes.

At some services, I've been given readings from various mediums. On one occasion my maternal grandfather, who passed away before I was born, advised me to finish my memoir. I was able to identify him through the medium's description.

The most profound experience happened some months after

Franny's passing. I questioned my care of Franny: Was it the best I could've done? What might I have done better to make her life more pleasant? I never discussed this with anyone and even felt guilty about it.

At the social gathering one Sunday, I was approached by the guest medium I hadn't seen before. She came up to me and gave me a big hug and a kiss on the cheek. She said to me, "Your wife says you did a great job!" WOW! I was stunned!

Then many months after Clemmy passed, during the readings, a different medium singled me out and shared, "A man in a wheelchair (who she described as short and hunched over) was very thankful you went to visit him every week." I knew it was Clemmy, and it made me feel like perhaps I may have at least done some things right.

Photo Gallery

20-ft Luger

22-ft Macgregor, Onset Bay

26-ft Balboa, nicknamed "The Clemon"

1987—Franny in the Balboa

Sailing on Balboa with Pete and Priscilla (and their granddaughters) in their catboat

1980—Franny at Camp Mullin

1995—House in Wareham

1962—Grace Gorman, my mother

1990—Clement V. Smith II, my father

1981—Fran, Mary, Becky, Clemmy, Greg, Richie, and Joe

1982—Greg, Rosemary Serson (Maureen's foster mom), Maureen, Franny

1983—Franny and Vaughn, Attleboro house

1983—John and Greg

1989—Back (L-R): Mary, Franny, Joel, Vaughn, Clemmy
Front (L-R): Fran, Joe, Greg, Maxi (dog), Richie, and Becky

1991—Ilse and Dad

1991—Franny at Becky and Andy's wedding, Camp Mullin

1992—Becky, Fran, Joel, and Mary

1993—Vaughn, Franny, Julia (Ilse's niece), Ilse, and Joel

Walker Camp in Maine

1993—Clemmy and Franny

1993—John, Maureen, and Gail

2002—Clemmy with Corey Kent Award

2002—Day of presentation of Clemmy's award
Becky, Mary, Fran, Clemmy, Joe, Richie, Greg, Franny, and Vaughn

2005—Greg, Maureen, Becky, and Joe

2005—Rob and Maureen

2006—Grandkids: Michelina, Joel, Emma, Genevieve, and Gwen

2009—Clemmy, Joe, Greg, and Richie

2012—Vaughn and Franny on La Dolce Vita, Narragansett Bay

2012—Vaughn and Franny, Thanksgiving

Our Last Family Photo
2016—Joel and Brittany's Wedding, Jefferson, NH
Back (L-R): Chrystal, Rich, Greg, Vaughn, Becky, Andy,
Jim, Joe, Mary, Wally
Middle (L-R): Gwen, Emma, Genevieve, Fran, Michelina, Egidia
Front (L-R): Malcolm, Joel, Clemmy, Franny, Brittany

2018—Greg, Gail, and John

2021—Johnny (Gorman), Sydni, Greg, and Vaughn, Cape Cod Canal

2021—Grampy and grandkids, Provincetown, MA
Gwen, Michelina, Vaughn, Malcom, and Emma

Epilogue

WHILE MY LIFE WAS IN PROCESS, I DIDN'T REALIZE how great and joyful it was. Now that I have the perspective of recalling my great and blessed life, what are the feelings with which I'm left?

For my early life, I feel sympathy for my parents and especially my brother. It may seem strange to some, but I've always felt love for those folks. Their lives must not have been happy. I feel blessed I was able to build a happy and fulfilling life.

I was divinely guided and blessed with talent and success as a self-educated engineer. I'm most grateful for Franny, our family, and the wonderful and happy life I've had. The great gift of Franny and her brilliant management and remarkable success in guiding our children to successful lives makes me truly, truly thankful to the Creator. I may have helped, but she was the driving force, guiding light, and my inspiration.

Marrying Franny was the best thing that ever happened to me: divine guidance all the way. To find my perfect mate was truly a great blessing.

I have to say, I have few regrets. Yes, there are things I could've done, and on reflection they may have improved some things. I could've made more money. Would this have improved the end results? This is unknowable. To me, it's clear the results were good, even great!

As I see it, life is made up of many small parts and details. Often a small change to a little detail can have a big impact. An example is how I met Franny. If I'd gone to dinner, we never would've met. Had Franny followed her usual pattern of behavior on that night, we never would've met. Wow! What were the odds? The explanation is divine guidance. I'm very grateful to my divine guide, whoever that may be. I've had a long, happy life and spent most of it with a very special partner. The resulting legacy is, I think, one of success. I'm very, very proud of Franny, all the Smith kids, and even myself.

Since Franny's passing, there's a prayer I say aloud twice every day. It goes like this:

"To the Creator, I give thanks for all my present and past blessings. I'm especially grateful for the gift of 58 years with my Franny Girl, our great, great family, and the wonderful, wonderful gift of me being able to take care of Franny for the last year and a half or so of her life and hold her hand as she passed. I'm also grateful for the gift from the Creator in the form of a talent that allowed me to support our family. For all these gifts, and my happy early formative years, I'm truly, truly, truly grateful.

It is my wish that those souls which have passed receive a special blessing: Franny Girl, Clemmy, Joe Mullin, Richie Mullin, Bill Mullin, Joe Mullin Jr., and Trudy Nightingale (the complete list is much longer).

It is also my wish that those who are ill, will improve: Pam and Shea, Brad Berit, and Gerry Mullin (this also is only a partial list, but I think you get the idea), and all others in need of such help.

It is also my wish that those seeking new and improved employment will succeed in their quest. May they all prosper.

It is also my wish that our President and legislators come together and restore this country to financial stability, and that in the future our leaders show wisdom so there is peace in the world.

It is also my wish that the COVID pandemic, which continues to negatively affect us all, will end sooner rather than later.

I hope the Creator will look upon me with favor and grant me these wishes. Amen."

Acknowledgements

THIS PROJECT WAS A GREAT EXPERIENCE FOR ME. FIRST, I'd like to thank Julie Saunders, my granddaughter, Gwen Walsh, and Irene Barron for their help typing up my notes early on in the process. The hardest parts, that took the most time and work, were the rewrites, formatting, and final editing. I'm very, very grateful to my daughter-in-law, Egidia Vergano, and her able assistant, my granddaughter, Michelina Smith, both of whom are much better writers than I am. Without their contributions it wouldn't have been as good or complete. Egidia was aware of much of the Smith Family history and jogged my memory, providing many worthwhile additions. My style is rather blunt and flat. I give her credit for smoothing out the bumps and making it readable. Egidia also leaned on me to improve accuracy. She was very patient and spent many, many hours working with me. I must, once again, express my thanks and gratitude for her hard work. Thanks also to Marianne Vergano-Laughton for assisting with the final editing.

All errors of fact are mine, my excuse just being an elderly guy with a faulty and selective memory.

About the Author

CLEMENT SMITH IS A SELF-EDUCATED MECHANICAL ENGI-
neer. He grew up in a tumultuous household, living in five
states and three countries until his freshman year in high
school when his family settled in Stoughton, Massachusetts. Despite
the difficulties of his childhood, he went on to achieve career success
and marry the love of his life with whom he spent 60 years and raised
seven children. He lives in Wareham, Massachusetts and enjoys spending time with his family.

Made in the USA
Middletown, DE
23 July 2022

69875289R00106